Prepare to be Judged

How to Get Your Car Ready for Show

Ron Peters

16 Ton Press

Prepare to be Judged

Copyright © 2011 by 16 Ton Press

All rights reserved. No part of this book may be reproduced or transmitted in any form or by any means, electronic or mechanical, including photocopying, recording, or by any information storage and retrieval system, without written permission from the publisher, except for the inclusion of brief quotations in a review.

ISBN: 978-0-557-76840-0

Trademarks

All terms mentioned in this book that are known to be trademarks or service marks have been appropriately capitalized. Use of a term in this book should not be regarded as affecting the validity of any trademark or service mark. All other trademarks are the property of their respective owners.

Disclaimer

This book is designed to provide information that is accurate and authoritative in regard to the subject matter covered. Every effort has been made to make this book as complete and as accurate as possible, but no warranty or fitness is implied.

The information is provided on an as-is basis. The author and 16 Ton Press shall have neither liability nor responsibility to any person or entity with respect to any loss or damages arising from the information contained in this book.

Table of Contents

Introduction 7
What It's All About 7
How This is Written 9
Who Should Read This 9
Details 10
Judging 12
Most Importantly 16

Body 19
Hood / Trunk / Top 19
Body Panels 21
Paint 22
Panel Fit 26
Accessories 29
Grille / Trim 30
Headlights / Taillights / Marker Lights 32
Customized Body 34

Interior 37
Windows 38
Trim / Weatherstripping 40
Seating / Panels / Headliner 41
Dash / Console 45
Instrumentation and Electrical 45
Floor Covering 47
Trim and Bright Work 48
Trunk / Bed 49
Convertible Top 53

Engine 55
Authenticity 56
Wiring 58
Plumbing 62
Plating and Bright Work 63
Detail 64
Installation and Engineering 65
Firewall / Engine Bay 65

Chassis 69
Wheels / Tires (Detailed / Indexed) 70
Suspension, Steering / Brakes, Rear-end 74
Frame and the Rest of the Underside 74

Presentation 79
Judge's Book 80
Story Board 83
Participants Interview 85
Innovation, Concept & Execution 87
Display 87

Location 90
Category Notes.. 92

How to Improve 93
How is the Event Judged... 93
Score Sheets 94
Talk with the Judges.. 95
Evaluate Your Score.. 95
Second Set of Eyes.. 96
Location Location Location.. 97
Learn More... 97
Top Down Approach 98

Hosting a Clinic 101
What are the Benefits 102
What to Include... 103
When to have the Clinic.. 104
Organization.. 105

Sample Score Sheet..................................... 107
Usage.. 107
Body.. 107
Paint 108
Engine 108
Chassis 108
Interior... 109
Safety 109
Display 109
Pointers 110

Afterword 111

Introduction

What It's All About

This book is intended to bring to light the judging process and how to prepare your car to maximize your standings as well as present your car in the best way possible. Like most of you, I've been judging car shows for most of my life, only not in an official capacity. All vehicles I see are run through the filters of how cool it is, its stance, build quality, historical significance, and rarity among many other criteria. It's part of being a certified gear head. For the last few years however, I've been officially judging at some of the local hot rod shows. What I learned, now that I am applying a formalized set of standards, is that most of the participants have some idea of how they should prepare their vehicle but don't seem to understand the full extent of what the judges look for or how they approach their job.

Most people showing a car understand that their vehicle should be cleaned, shined, polished, and detailed. However, when that

Prepare To Be Judged

car, truck, or motorcycle is put under the judging microscope, many fall short of what they could accomplish simply by not focusing closely enough on the details. There is a big difference between what they feel is "good enough to win" versus what the judges are really looking for in an outstanding vehicle.

You might think, as I originally did, that the owners of highly customized and expensive vehicles would already understand all of this, as in many cases they are professional builders or have been to many shows. While this is mostly true, I have found that there are very few high-end vehicles where I wasn't able to quickly find something that should have been easily remedied and would have increased their standing with the judges.

The techniques here will be useful even if you are attending a non-judged event such as a cruise night at a local pizza joint. The goal is for a triple win. You will maximize your vehicle so you can enjoy and show it off more, the show spectators and other participants will get a better show whether they've paid or not and finally, the show promoter now has a better class of cars which will draw more spectators and participants for future shows and the cycle continues.

Not all shows are judged with a standardized scoring system. In fact there are many different methods of show judging depending on the type and size of show. There are hot rod shows at local convention centers and fairgrounds, organized cruise-ins both open and manufacturer specific, concours events, and impromptu gatherings among others. Some of these have specific and highly detailed rules for competition, others simply have a few people who walk around and choose the cars they like best and the whole continuum in between. If you're in it for the competition, it is best to determine in advance what your show is about and tailor your methods suit your needs. The focus of this book is mainly on hot rod type shows but most of the techniques and points of information can be applied to all types of shows.

I'd like to highlight one particular type of show that is a bit different. Concours D'elegance judging is an animal unto itself. Many of the techniques discussed here will apply but the real

Introduction

focus at these shows is on factory originality, provenance, and historical significance. No matter the type of vehicle you have, there is likely a club or other organization that is well versed in concours shows and can point you in the right direction. The judges are usually highly qualified in their field with the most minute details being scrutinized for originality. Some classes of vehicles and their associated clubs have very detailed and specific rules and standards that if followed, will make your vehicle factory fresh. Others simply rely on the knowledge of the experts and whatever pictures and documentation can be found. The focus of concours judging is really outside the scope of this book.

How This is Written

This book is broken up into a number of chapters, each related to a category that will be judged. In each chapter, I will focus on that category and highlight ways to improve your standing. The chapter following the judging categories ties all the previous ones together and discusses many ways that you can improve beyond the specific items being judged on your vehicle. The final chapter discusses how to host a show preparation clinic. This is useful for show promoters who would like to help their participants perform better. Finally, I've included a sample score sheet to use where you can apply your new understanding to your vehicle and use that knowledge for future improvement.

Who Should Read This

Initially, when I started this project, I focused on the show participant who has a nice car but may be a novice at scored events. This book will help those that have never had to be measured against other cars or a standard other than the casual observer at the local cruise night.

What I've found is that this book should be read and applied at all levels of show participants no matter their experience. Many shows have a number of headliner cars that may or may not be professionally built and put onto the show circuit. These are very expensive and incredibly beautiful vehicles. Until I was able to get a close look at some of these vehicles, I would have never thought they would need a guide like this. Don't get me wrong, I'm not saying that these types of cars only have a quality that is skin deep and that they aren't built with care. The truth is that they are incredible works of art and engineering and from most angles, even close up, they are amazing.

What I am saying is that there are details overlooked at all levels and the top notch cars are not immune. One of the problems with some of the details that aren't attended to on the high end cars is that those problems stand out more when the rest of the quality is so high. Another common issue is simple detail misses that were just overlooked. Reading through this book and adjusting your focus on details will help you dial in and focus more clearly on a methodical process of inspecting your car.

Details

I once had a Track and Field coach who said that meets are determined by fractions of inches and tenths of seconds. Car shows are much the same in that the competition can be very close and giving a little more focused effort can be the determining factor between not placing and taking top honors.

One of the classes in a recent show had a very close race for first place. The judges were at an impasse as both cars were very evenly matched. The cars and their scores were reviewed multiple times to determine a final result. After much discussion, one of the cars was finally given the win because the other vehicle was found to have a light layer of dust on the top of the engine supporting cross member. This was a 5-10 second wipe down which would have forced the judges to continue looking for a determining difference.

> "Every part of the car is the car, starting from the frame, when we put it on the floor, it is finished as if it will be the focal point of the car and every part that gets bolted to the frame is treated that way."
> - Chip Foose referring to the build process of the 2005 Ridler award winning 'Impression'.

Introduction

In other words, attention is given to every part of the car no matter how seemingly insignificant as if it were the central feature. Foose has clearly demonstrated his focus and level of detail by winning the Ridler award multiple times. I had an opportunity to inspect the car 'Impression' at one of the shows I judged though I didn't judge that car. Being a judge allows you to get closer to the vehicles than most so I spent the time lying beneath the car staring at the wonderfully crafted chassis. The car was phenomenal in its detail. It was clearly better than anything I've ever seen. There are so many aspects of that car that would never be seen unless viewed from all angles.

There are a couple of common phrases relating to the details within a project. "The Devil is in the details" and "God is in the details." I prefer the latter for at least two reasons. First, it is more optimistic and second, because when you focus on the details, the quality increases. The former phrase implies that getting all the details right is an arduous and painful task. I hope that working on your pride and joy isn't a burden and that you actually enjoy your hobby. The latter phrase suggests that when the details are focused on and attended to, the result is something wonderful.

In any case, preparing for a show is an effort in focusing on the details. There are plenty of cars that look nice driving down the road or even when walking by but could use some help when you get close. You've potentially spent hundreds if not thousands of hours and more money than you probably ever intended to get your car to a particular level. Make the extra effort and finish strong even if it is only to satisfy your own obsessive nature.

There are a lot of topics that I cover in a fair amount of detail on what you should do to present your car in the best way possible. I don't necessarily specify how to perform those tasks. For instance, when detailing an interior, there are many types of materials found in an interior including metal, plastic, cloth, leather, rubber, and others, all of which need to be cleaned. I leave it to you to find the best method for your application.

The good news about many of the topics that are discussed is that they either don't cost much or are simple to implement. The vast majority are simply detailing (cleaning) items. Some are presentation items relating to how the car is displayed. There are also some hints to note that may help overcome shortcomings of your vehicle. Most of the rest are items of quality that may cost more than a nominal amount to remedy. If you're still in the process of building your car, you may want to take note of all the items here as the pre-planning may help down the road.

One final note on working out the details. Preparing for a show can be a stressful and harried affair or it can be a relaxing and fulfilling event. I know that planning ahead and having the uninterrupted time to really detail my car is an excellent escape from daily life. Sometimes it takes a bit of effort to get started, but the journey is its own reward. For those of us gear-heads that really love our car, the time can fly by and it can be a mini-vacation from our normal routine. The resulting benefit of driving your freshly detailed machine is that you have this fresh clean sense, like the car is new all over again. I read an article many years ago that made the claim that washing your car is the most intimate and sensual time you can have with it. You're able to inspect and feel every inch and gain a truly physical bond with the vehicle and its design. This may sound odd but I suspect you will hear the ring of truth.

Judging

As I've already mentioned, there are numerous types of shows in which you can participate. One of the things to remember about a judged show is ultimately, even though there may be scoring rules and guidelines, the judges are human and they all have some level of subjectivity. They have specific tastes and pet peeves, likes and dislikes. They may have had a bad day or hate/love your type of vehicle regardless of the rest of the class. Even with these elements, quality workmanship will be evident. This is the main reason I like events that score the vehicles by a standard. The entrants are judged on more of an even playing field than with simple open class events. When vehicles are

Introduction

judged by a standard, quality becomes more valuable to the results than flashy paint or a big blower.

Scoring methods can be based on 1000 points or some other arbitrarily chosen top possible score and the points are then decremented based on how much the standard is missed. Another scoring method is to assign points for each item within a category where each category weighs the same. Bonus points may be given for originality or showmanship or simply at the judges discretion. Some other systems use club favorites, sponsor's choice, people's choice, top 5, and many more. There are pros and cons to all of these and I'm going to stay away from any comparison. The focus here is to stick to a plan for preparation no matter the type of show.

A code of ethics should exist for judges whether official or not. These are my rules and not necessarily a standard or possible in all situations but they are an excellent starting point: A judge should avoid scoring their own car or even being nearby when it is being scored. A judge shouldn't score a car of someone they know (friend or foe) to avoid any perception of partiality. A judge should keep good notes on their score sheet in the event that someone questions how or why they were scored in a certain way.

One rule that all judges should adhere to is to be sensitive and discrete with specific information. The conversations about vehicles that are being compared to the perfect standard can be harsh and potentially disturbing to the owner of the vehicle. This isn't a personal attack, just the job of the judge. Subjective commentary, if any, about vehicles should be kept within the confines of the judge's private conversations as these comments can damage reputations of both individuals and the show itself. It's the same as the old adage of "loose lips sink ships." The job of the judge is to present an objective score based on predetermined criteria. Hopefully, all the shows you enter are held to this standard.

The judges may or may not be able to touch the car during judging. This is often due to liability issues but it just good

Prepare To Be Judged

practice as you never know what type of mechanical quirks a given vehicle may have. I have heard of an incident where a judge simply opened a door on a car to view the jam and the door fell off. The judge doesn't want to be in that position.

The judges may synchronize themselves if there are multiple groups that are judging different vehicles within the same class. This is so they can align their scoring process for the rest of the class and keep the judging as fair as possible. If there are vehicles that score very closely in a class, the judges may switch vehicles and re-score to make sure that their thoughts and scores are aligned.

If there are vehicles in a class that score out of the top three but are somewhat close, special care should be taken to annotate details on the score sheet specifying why the vehicle was given specific scores. There are some participants that take the judging very seriously and can get quite upset if they don't win or have the perception that they were slighted in some way.

Many times during the judging process, questions like these are asked: "What is it about this particular body/interior/etc that makes it less than perfect?" or "How does this vehicle compare to the last vehicle we judged in the same category?". This helps the judges weigh all the vehicles equally. They may return and re-assess portions of previously judged vehicles based on judging that comes later in the process. The judges try their best to keep all the vehicles in the specific class they are judging in mind so they can be as consistent as possible with their scoring.

One of the biggest questions among participants is in which class their vehicle best fits. The combinations are endless. The number of classes are broad and they change from year to year. The types of vehicles are nearly infinite. Your class choice may be purely up to you depending on the type of show you enter. In some shows, you'll probably narrow down the possible classes you best fit, but the staff may move your vehicle to another class for various reasons. There may not be enough vehicles to warrant a separate class. Your vehicle may actually score better in a different class. This is all show dependent.

Introduction

Often times there are multiple class definitions so familiarize yourself with the show's classifications to best position your vehicle. I've seen a number of beautifully presented cars fail to place because they were in the wrong class. Features of the car become scoring detriments. Wonderfully modified cars are scored down against a stock class and a perfectly restored car will place poorly against cars in a performance or customized class. Some shows have guidelines that will specify what constitutes being in a specific class. It is wise to follow these to best compete.

The judging process itself will vary from show to show. Some shows are judged at night when the owners and crowds are not around. This allows the judges to be candid and free with their comments. Some shows will have the owner participate so they have an opportunity to give as much information to the judges as possible, however, this is all dependent on the show.

Shows may have some type of identification marker indicating a vehicle has been judged such as a sticker on a headlight or the corner of the windshield. There are times however that even though your vehicle has been judged it may be viewed again by the judges. In some cases, there are very close competitions and your vehicle may be scrutinized a number of times before the end of the show. Take every possible opportunity to have your vehicle viewed in the most positive light by the judges.

There may be situations where you will have special needs or requests. Don't think that you are out of luck because many times the show staff will help as much as they can. Send a note or talk to the show staff for any special requests (within reason). For instance, if you forgot to leave your vehicle open for judging and it was judged, ask if you can have another chance with the vehicle open. Another instance I've run into is that a vehicle received some damage when it was moved into the show arena as well as a tire that was going flat. The owner asked if the judges could keep those items in the proper light and that the owner was aware of the defects and did all they could. The staff and judges of the events are generally willing to work with you and want you to perform as well as possible without giving special treatment.

Most shows will not only have guidelines about how the show is to be judged or how the vehicles are placed in classes, in many cases there will be certain rules to follow for various other reasons. Some are logistical as in when and how the vehicles can be moved in or out, when the show times start and how long it goes, when the judging is held, and trophies are handed out. Some are safety related such as limiting the amount of fuel on board, disconnecting the battery, or sealing off the fuel filler. These are all important and you should make yourself aware of how your particular show functions.

This last note on the judging process is very important and should be remembered. What a judge doesn't see, whether it is because they couldn't or it was simply missed, doesn't exist. In other words, if your vehicle has a notably good or bad detail that the judges don't see, you won't be given appropriate points or deductions. This can be good or bad for the entrant. If you have a flaw, and you can make that flaw disappear by way of covering it or by some other means, the judge cannot score you down for it. If, on the other hand, you have an excellent detail, but it is covered by something so it is not visible, you won't receive beneficial scoring. Keep in mind that the judges will try to see as much as they possibly can to give the most fair and accurate score they can. They will likely crawl around as far as they can to get under or around the vehicle and view it from all angles. They will also use various tools such as flashlights or mirrors to view hard-to-reach areas.

The take home message of all of these details is that for whatever show or competition you enter, it is beneficial to find out how the judging is performed so you can be ready and prepare appropriately.

Most Importantly

The most important part of any show is that you should have fun. There are those that are presenting cars for business purposes

Introduction

such as vendors and this book will be valuable for them. But my focus is on the individual who is showing their vehicle for fun as part of their hobby and wants to put their best foot forward.

Be as obsessive as your personality can take. Don't go overboard and make the preparation a job that is held with contempt. This hobby is about having fun and meeting great people with similar interests. Don't take it too seriously. Keep in mind that your car is likely being compared to a mythical perfect standard somewhere in the distance and don't feel bad when you aren't scored perfectly in all areas. Take the opportunity to learn from the experience and use the information to come back next time and perform better.

Along those lines, the end goal is to enhance your car to be the best it can be, not necessarily to get the $20 trophy. Accolades are nice, but aren't worth making a stink because you feel you should have done better and that the judges should have picked your vehicle for the top prize. I have run into a lot of folks with big delicate egos who can't seem to handle constructive criticism or that their car isn't the best thing since sliced bread. This is a problem whenever you have functions involving people.

Be friendly and courteous, take your licks and be a man (so to speak). Come back next time with improvements and compete like everyone else. Being a mean complainer won't win you any awards. Go easy on the judges, they're enthusiasts too. Judges love their jobs for the same reason you love your car or truck. They want to see the cool vehicles and it is their passion. Treat them with respect and dignity.

Prepare To Be Judged

Body

In many ways, the body is the most important part of your vehicle. It not only determines the make and model of your vehicle but the overall look that will be presented to spectators and ultimately for the judges. The body is also the first part of the car that is seen and defines the first impression that you only get once. Keep in mind that in terms of judging, the category of the body is examined separately from the paint although those two features are intimately tied together. The quality of the body will be magnified by the paint both good and bad.

Unfortunately, the quality of many of the items covered in this chapter are determined at the time the vehicle is originally restored, fabricated, or assembled but there are areas that you can maximize. If you are at the point of building your latest project, these are good points to consider.

Hood / Trunk / Top

The most visible parts of the the body are the upper most flat

Prepare To Be Judged

and expansive surfaces. These are the locations where the light most readily reflects and what the casual observer (including yourself) sees as the highlight of the vehicle. It's one thing to have a small one inch ding in the rocker panel which is more or less out of sight, but another all together to have that same ding in the middle of an otherwise perfectly straight hood. These panels are scrutinized more closely when being judged for this reason. They are also more simple to judge because the reflected light is easier to use as a tool to look across the large panels and view imperfections, waves, and any unevenness. As stated before, the quality of the body panels is determined at the time when the bodywork is performed. If you're at that point, make sure you or your shop pays extra attention to these areas even if only to satisfy yourself. Once you find any defect, you'll be more sensitive to it even if it is never noticed by anyone else.

Illustration 1: This convertible is displayed with the top up allowing the judges to fully inspect the vehicle.

Convertible and rag tops are wonderful features and can make a rare vehicle even more enjoyable and possibly more valuable. Many times the vehicle will present better with the top down, showing the vehicle in all its freedom loving glory. Unfortunately, the top cannot be effectively judged while it is down. When the top is up, the judges are able to inspect all aspects including the cloth, rear window, mechanicals, headliner, trim and bright work including any attachment mechanisms.

Body

If the show you're attending is judged at a different time than when the spectators view the vehicles, then you have the opportunity for the best of both worlds. During show hours, present the vehicle so that it is viewed best. During judging hours, adjust your vehicle so that the judges get their view and you have the best opportunity for scoring well. The downside is having to readjust your vehicle potentially multiple times during a show. Of course the readjustment of your vehicle won't apply for shows where the judging is performed during the time when spectators are in attendance. Find out in advance how and when the judging is performed at your particular show so you can maximize your impact and score.

Body Panels

Next in importance to the upper parts of the body are the side panels. All of these will enhance or detract from the initial impression. The panels being the fenders, doors, quarter panels, rocker panels, and lower front and rear valances. Depending on the vehicle, the number of panels may be more, less or just different such as with a truck, convertible, or open wheeled vehicle. In any case, these panels, like the top surfaces, are judged for straightness and body line. The judge will be

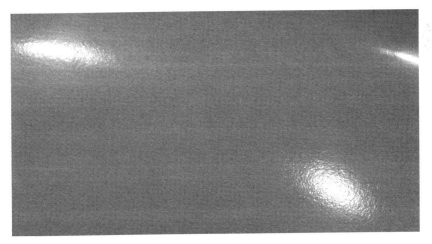

Illustration 2: You can see that this paint texture could be improved possibly with color sanding.

checking for dents, dings, and creases along with any other panel deformity.

Your vehicle will be inspected for signs of panel replacement, consistency from side to side of the vehicle and evenness of the panel seams. This is the fit and finish of the body. The judjes will also look for body repair that isn't performed to a high standard. This will be indicated by a panel that is uneven in a particular area or wavy panels that should be flat. Viewing reflections of straight lines such as a tubular fluorescent shop light down the side of a vehicle will easily show the quality of the body.

Another judged aspect is any underlying body repair that can be seen by means of sanding marks, pinholes of improperly sealed body filler, or areas of the body that don't quite have the same quality as the surrounding area. Other signs of body issues can be seen in areas that may be notorious for rust such as rocker panels, lower quarter panels, and 'A' and 'C' pillars (especially with vinyl tops). These issues can be seen by either rust bubbles coming through the paint or smooth body filler bubbles pushing the paint up where the filler is coming away from the body.

Most of this is determined when the body and paint work are performed or when the initial build takes place but there are techniques and professional services for removing dents without damaging paint (depending on severity), or making small body repairs and blending them with their surroundings. You can also have fenders, doors, and hood readjusted for better alignment without too much trouble or expense though you may need to get an expert to help.

Paint

The condition of the paint is intimately connected with the condition of the body. It is the skin that gives the body it's character, color, emotion, pizazz, and finishing touch that covers the more industrial look of bare metal finishes. There are many items to consider when judging the paint. The overall condition, as many in the automotive hobby are aware of, can be stated in

Body

Illustration 3: Notice the incredible depth and shine of this paint.

terms of distance. This is where the distance denotes how far you have to stand away from the vehicle before the paint looks good. The 50' paint job is dramatically different from the 5" paint job. The flatness of the paint, the depth of the shine, the consistency of the metal flake are just some of the characteristics of paint that will be investigated.

The depth and clarity of the shine in the paint can be enhanced with a technique called color sanding. This technique involves a lot of work as well as knowledge of the paint that is applied to your vehicle. A good indicator of the shine quality is to view the reflection of some type of very straight edge in the paint and determine the quality of that image. A fluorescent tube light is a good example since it is bright and straight. When viewing the image in the paint, if the straight edges of the reflected image have a rough appearance and aren't clear, this is where you'll want to focus your attempts at improvement.

Color sanding is a technique where you use very fine sand paper

23

Prepare To Be Judged

with a block to smooth the paint to a perfectly even and level surface. You should give a lot of thought and research to this before attempting as you can easily ruin your paint. A painted surface may shine well enough, but if you look closely, as with the aid of the reflected tube or some other light source, you'll likely see minor imperfections and bumps and valleys known as 'orange peel'. The ultra-fine grit sand paper flattens the bumps to a perfectly smooth finish but it also removes the shine. After the sanding is complete, the paint is then buffed with various finishing compounds and buffing pads to restore the shine to a mirror-like finish. Make sure that you have enough paint or clear coat thickness to be able to remove the imperfections without burning through the coating. This is where the research and experience come into play. It may be more effective and safer to have this performed by a professional.

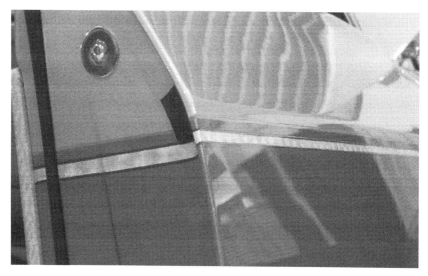

Illustration 4: High design detail can be seen in this door jam where the exterior scheme is followed though to the inside of the door.

Along with the overall quality of paint, the judges will look for nicks, scratches, mismatched or discolored areas, even metallic distribution if that applies, runs and drips, orange peel, over spray, and under spray. All of these items could detract from the score and a quality paint job. The vehicle will be inspected in as

Body

many areas as can be seen which may include hidden areas in door, hood, or trunk jams, frame rails, and wheel wells. In shows where the judges are allowed to physically touch the vehicles, they may run their fingers along areas that cannot be seen to determine the level of detail that the builder maintained. At high levels of competition, these are the details that can affect the final results.

Illustration 5: Custom graphics such as flames can be performed with a high level of skill like these. They show depth with their over and under design.

Other areas that are viewed closely are any custom paint or graphics that have been applied. This can be judged for originality, quality, and overall theme. Any graphics that are on the vehicle will be judged for authenticity if in a stock class, quality of application, as well as level of difficulty used for the effect. Certain types of graphic finishes can be extremely difficult

Illustration 6: The paint behind this emblem has been detailed so that no residual cleaning agents are visible.

to pull off well and those that succeed will be rewarded.

The last item related to the paint is the one that the owner can have the most impact, which is the detail of preparation. The paint should be polished to a high sheen but without polishing marks. All jams including the hood, cowl, trunk and door areas should be as clean as the outside of the body.

There should be no polishing residue visible in any area of the vehicle including any rubber or plastic areas, within any panel gaps, vent grooves, or emblems. The body should be inspected closely throughout so that all unwanted material is removed. This may be where you clean with micro fiber cloths and cotton swabs to get that perfect clean.

Panel Fit

As you get closer to the vehicle after the initial view of the body and paint, a more detailed inspection of the body fit and finish gives telltale signs of what lies beyond. It can indicate the type of quality control the factory employs when the vehicle was originally built or it can show that a vehicle has had some sort

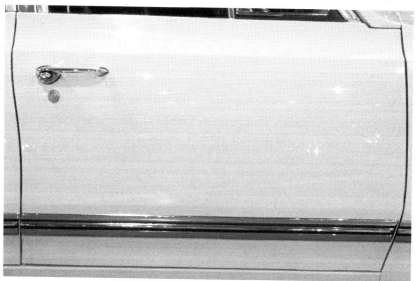

Illustration 7: The gaps here are aligned evenly all around the door.

of damage which may be as minimal as a bump in a parking lot or major damage that doesn't allow the panels to fit correctly without some sort of frame or chassis repair.

In the case of show vehicles, along with the previous reasons, panel fit can show the craftsmanship of the one who re-assembled the vehicle during a restoration. When judging, these indicators will give you signs of quality that you may see again during further examination of other components of the vehicle. This can be true in both positive and negative terms.

Illustration 8: The gaps on this door are much wider near the hinges than the jam. Also, the trim on the rear of the door doesn't quite match the trim on the rear quarter.

The key to panel fit, presenting not performing, is that the panels should be even. This means even in all respects. Take note of the gaps between panels. They should be the same width from beginning to end. For instance, the hinge side gap on a door that is wider at the top may indicate that the door is hanging low and either needs to be adjusted or have hinge work.

The gap should also be the same width on all sides of a panel such as the hinge and striker side of a door or all sides of a hood (bonnet in Britain) or trunk lid (boot). This may be a difficult task on some vehicles as the tolerances originally from the factory weren't very good. As a student of your particular vehicle, you'll be able to determine what the proper widths should be by comparison with other restored examples.

The next gap to even out is from side to side. The doors should not only be even all the way around, but should have the same gap on both sides of the vehicle. This is true for all gaps that are similar from one side of the vehicle to the other.

Illustration 9: Panels of varying levels can be seen in this example.

Another adjustment to watch for is how level the panel is compared to its surrounding panels. When a door closes, both ends of the door should be at the same level as their nearest panel. If the panels aren't adjusted properly, the door can look as if it is not completely closed or closed too far and sunken into the surrounding body. There should be no abrupt level changes from panel to panel.

The last item is the overall fit in regards to trim and body line alignment. Most vehicles have trim or design features that span the entire vehicle. These should be aligned so the transition from one panel to the next is only noticed by the gap between them. Like the panels themselves, the trim pieces should be aligned so that when viewing down the side of a vehicle, no abrupt changes from piece to piece are noticed.

Getting the panel fit right can be an extremely tedious process. As I mentioned previously, it can indicate underlying damage much like a wall can never be repaired correctly if the foundation is cracked or out of line. Some vehicles may not have much variability in the adjustments for gap fit. Going beyond simple adjustments and taking more extreme measures may be in order. Fit the gaps as closely as possible with the existing adjustments and then take measurements to determine where more adjustments are required. At this point you may need to add or remove material to get the measurements perfect by welding on additional metal or grinding down portions to keep the proper distance. This is probably the last resort on most vehicles but will continue to push the vehicle down the road approaching perfection.

It is quite easy to neglect these details when you see the freshly applied paint and your vehicle glows like it never has before, but you'll be glad you took the time when the body lines are perfect. This is a detail that isn't highly noticeable unless it is performed poorly. These are things you should watch for when you or your shop assembles the vehicle.

Accessories

Accessories will vary from vehicle to vehicle depending on how many features are equipped on the particular car. These can range from an optional passenger side mirror to fender mounted turn signal markers to tinted glass to a bumper mounted winch. These are generally optional or add-on equipment that makes the vehicle more 'special' than others of its kind. This is an area that may give an opportunity to add some points to your score by adding additional features to the vehicle. It is also possible that the judges won't recognize all of the special features of your vehicle. These are some things that would be excellent additions

Prepare To Be Judged

to the documentation in your judge's book. I'll discuss this more in the chapter on presentation.

Grille / Trim

The focus of the trim and bright work category is in the quality of the pieces. These include any body side moldings, grille, window trim, bumpers, and anything else that is external ornamentation in a metal finish or contrasting color. A judge will evaluate how straight and smooth the pieces are accounting for any scratches, dings, dents, or misalignments. Some grilles have quite ornate designs that are fairly delicate in construction. Repairing any of these defects makes a nice grille perfect.

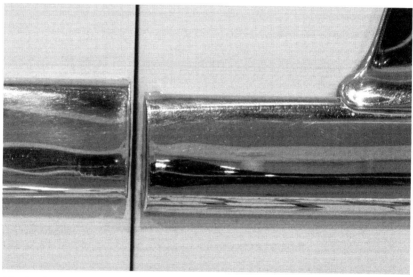

Illustration 10: The adjustment of these trim pieces could be improved.

The trim should be installed straight and align properly to the body, glass, paint, or adjacent trim pieces. The pieces should be clean especially where there are deep grooves and designed textures that will catch and hold onto dirt and polishing compounds. Another place for dirt and wax to build up is between the trim and the body or glass. Care should be taken to clean these areas thoroughly. One method to ensure that all is clean is to remove the trim from the vehicle and clean the underlying body and the less accessible parts of the trim itself. This also may help accessing hard to reach locations on the body such as behind the bumpers.

Illustration 11: The finish on this trim piece has been polished to an extremely high sheen.

The finish quality of the trim may be judged separately from the trim itself where the focus is on condition and installation. The scrutiny of the finish is very similar although the focus is a bit different. Scoring high in this category is a result of hard work that really pays off. Polishing the trim to get an even, high quality mirror like shine is difficult and time consuming, but if you want to make the trim pop, it is worth the effort. As with color sanding paint, stainless steel features can be sanded (very fine grit such as 4000) and polished to a super high gloss. Chrome work on the other hand should probably be redone if it is in need. Chrome that is checked or dull will stand out poorly against that nice fresh paint job. Once again, if the finish has been polished completely, make sure there isn't any polishing residue remaining for the judges to see.

I've judged a near perfect car that was painstakingly prepared and since it was so nearly perfect, I looked very hard for any possible deductions. One of the very small number of deductions was with the grille cleanliness. The owner had missed some grime in the corner of the grille. This was a very small item, but had there been another vehicle of the same caliber, a small one point deduction for something so easy to remedy could have determined the difference in the competition.

Headlights / Taillights / Marker Lights

Headlights can be easily overlooked when preparing your vehicle. Many times the only attention they receive is when they need to be replaced or adjusted. This is yet another area that the judges scrutinize. The make and model of the lights should match from side to side. If there are four headlights, the manufacturer should be consistent for all four. The lights should be clean like everything else and at least close to being adjusted correctly as well as level in their orientation. If the vehicle is in a stock class, the lenses should match the vintage of the vehicle. Halogen headlamps weren't legal in the US until 1978 and then only sealed beams. It wasn't until 1983 when the use of non sealed beams were allowed in the US so use these types of lights appropriately.

Illustration 12: This lense could use a replacement.

Body

The taillights and marker lights should also be given close attention. The lenses and associated trim should be clean. This is especially evident in detail lines where grime can accumulate as well as between the lens and any associated trim or gasket seals. It is generally a simple matter of removing the lenses and giving them a good cleaning and polishing. There should be no wax or polishing residue visible in the creases. Cracks and nicks in the lenses will also deduct points as like-new condition is what matters here.

The color such as red or amber should be consistent on all lenses. This is sometimes difficult when parts are no longer reproduced or very hard to find. This being the case, there is another solution. There are companies that produce kits and materials for casting

Illustration 13: Notice the screws on this taillight are aligned in the same orientation both leaning toward the center of the vehicle.

your own lenses. The process is somewhat involved but generally not that difficult and produces high quality parts. The main requirement is that you have a perfectly shaped master to be copied.

When installing lenses, especially on older vehicles, mounting hardware such as the installation screws are often visible when the lens is installed. Another item that demonstrates your attention to detail is alignment of the screw heads so they match each other from light to light and screw to screw. Depending on the type of mounting screws, align them so they are visually pleasing such as horizontal or vertical. Another method with blade screws might be to align the heads on the right side at a 45 degree angle and the opposite angle on the left. This might be a nice complement to a vehicle and may need to be mentioned to the judge so they will take notice of your attention to detail.

I have seen this method used on an attached body panel that was scallop shaped with a flat end something like an air scoop. The panel was about a foot long and about half that wide. The blade screws secured the panel all the way around at about one inch intervals. The screws were oriented in such a way that the slots followed the shape of the curved scallop. The resulting installation displayed a very high level of competence and planning but probably wasn't an extremely difficult task.

Customized Body

Body modifications have been around as long as hot rods and have seen incredible advancements over the decades. For as long as this has been going on, the list of modifications has also been growing as well as the standard of quality to which they are being performed. A body can be chopped, channeled, sectioned, pancaked, frenched, flared, tucked, smoothed, narrowed, stretched, and scratch built, and these are only a few of the possible modifications. The possibilities are limited only by the imagination and budget of the owner or builder. One of the difficulties of judging body customizations is that when the quality of workmanship increases, the more challenging it

Body

is to recognize that modifications have been performed. This can also be difficult when the modification are very subtle but still difficult to perform. Judges will do their best to recognize the changes but it is wise to list and describe what has been performed in the judge's book that is discussed further in the Presentation chapter. Depending on the show, you may even have the opportunity to discuss the vehicle with the judge prior to them scrutinizing it. That would also be an excellent time to give as much information to them as possible to demonstrate the skill, level of workmanship, and difficulty factor in preparation of your vehicle. Once again, finding out all the details of how your show is run and the specifics of the judging process will definitely give you an advantage.

Prepare To Be Judged

Interior

In order of importance of the four overall components of the vehicle (body, interior, engine, and chassis), the interior is probably second on the list following the body and paint. The interior is what is viewed most closely followed by the engine compartment. This is where you and your passengers spend the most time. A casual observer seeing your vehicle on the street wouldn't be able to see the engine compartment and would probably look at the interior after admiring the body and paint. The preparation of the interior is important and is often ignored after the body, paint, and engine are complete. Don't get a false impression that only the driver cares about the quality of the interior or that the original interior is 'good enough'. Even though you may have a high quality original interior, this is no reason to only perform a cursory preparation or ignore it all together. The same attention to detail should be given to all aspects of the vehicle, not just what is easily visible from the outside.

Prepare To Be Judged

Windows

The windows are an interesting piece of a vehicle because they can be considered part of either the interior or exterior. It doesn't really matter how you classify them, as the judging is the same. I've arbitrarily chosen to include them with the interior. Also, in order of importance, the glass is the transition from the exterior of the vehicle to the interior so it makes sense that it is covered here.

Illustration 1: Note the water spots on this rear window. Some more detailing would help here.

There are several components to window judging. The first most obvious one is that they should be clean. You may be surprised at how many vehicles I've judged that have had issues in this area ranging from missing a small spot of dirt or fingerprint to glass that obviously hadn't been cleaned at all. The glass should be spotless which includes all hard to reach areas such as tight corners and edges. Whether the show is indoors or out, once you have cleaned the glass, try to view the windows from all angles with light sources both inside and out especially at sharp angles. This allows you to view the reflections from the surface of the

Interior

glass. The streaks will show up much better this way than when simply looking directly through the glass. Keep in mind that the interior materials can give off gases that may put a film onto the glass so if you know when judging takes place, it would be prudent to perform one final check or cleaning right before the appropriate time.

The second area that the judges look for relates to any damage the glass may have. Any nicks, chips, cracks, scratches, separation, and clouding. Replacement glass can be very expensive or non-existent without being custom made for some vehicles and a number of these issues can be repaired without purchasing new.

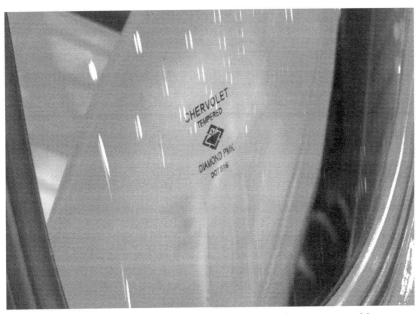

Illustration 2: Rear window with the proper manufacturers marking.

The manufacturer of the glass is another area that the judges may inspect. This is most important in factory stock classes since originality is key. The judge will validate that all of the windows have matching production markings. Any difference from one window to the next indicates a replacement with non-OEM parts and could potentially be a deduction.

The final item relates to the presentation of the glass to maximize your scoring potential. The judges can only judge what they can see and as I've said before, if they can't see 'it', the issue and its potential deduction don't exist. In the case of glass, if you have damaged or mis-matched glass, mainly side windows, strategically lowering the window that might give you the deduction may conceal those facts. If the judge can see some of the windows in full, the assumption in many cases is that the unseen ones are the same manufacturer and condition.

In some shows, this technique may not be effective as the judges may want to view all the windows in both up and down positions for cleanliness, quality, correctness, and functionality. This depends on the show that you enter and its particular rules. If you decide to lower all the windows so none of them are seen, you may lose points not because of flaws but because none of them are visible to be judged.

Trim / Weatherstripping

The trim and weatherstripping specific to the interior includes the pieces surrounding the inside of the windows and doors as well as any molding and rubber or plastic weatherstripping. This also includes vent window weatherstripping, rubber window scrapers and possibly window channel felt or what might be known as window fuzzies as well as the door sills.

Any weatherstripping should be attached correctly including hardware such as screws or clips. If attachment screws are visible, align their heads so they are oriented in the same direction. This is the kind of focus on detail that will be viewed favorably. The screw heads should have a new appearance and should not be covered in scratches, gouges, or chipping paint. The weatherstripping itself should be as clean as possible and show like new. Rubber and plastic items tend to show their age on vintage vehicles and their replacement is money well spent in both aesthetics and functionality.

Don't overlook side glass weatherstripping (window felt). It

Interior

should be cleaned if not replaced. This item is something that really stands out when not replaced on an otherwise high quality vehicle. I've seen many well detailed vehicles that have either missed or neglected this detail. For a judge, this feature is very easy to spot as it is right on the top of the door and readily visible.

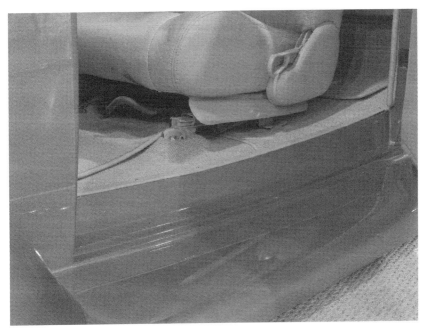

Illustration 3: Door sill and trim are of very high quality on this custom.

The door sills are easily overlooked especially when the doors are normally shut but these are what welcome you into the vehicle. Shiny paint and fresh carpet should be highlighted by either a new or heavily detailed sill. Both metal and plastic sills will often show lots of wear from years of use. Once again, align the heads of any visible mounting screws to focus on detail.

Seating / Panels / Headliner

The components of the interior that account for the majority of the surface area include the headliner, door and side panels, and the seats. These items will likely make up the quick first

Prepare To Be Judged

impression of the interior and should be detailed accordingly.

The headliner is an item that is easily overlooked because of the awkward motion it takes to look at as well as the fact they don't get much attention except in the case of the judges. Even though this is the case, the liner should be very clean and installed correctly. The cloth should be straight and pulled tight. I once saw a magazine article that demonstrated how to install your own headliner and the photo of the finished job showed a liner that wasn't tight and had kinks and wrinkles in multiple places. This isn't the way to impress the judges.

The judges will look at the quality of the door, side, and kick panels for installation and cleanliness. Consider removing all the panels and clean behind the edges wherever visible. These areas can be easily missed when detailing the interior. Also make sure that any pattern details or deep crevice such as an inset door handle is well cleaned. Some handles are surface mounted making them a bit easier to clean while others are molded into the shape of the panel and create a pocket for dirt and grime to accumulate.

Illustration 4: The seats in this interior are positioned well to match each other.

Interior

The seats should be very clean and aligned with one another. Look for any loose or frayed threads that may need to be repaired or trimmed. With adjustable seats, the driver and passenger seats should be adjusted so they appear in the same orientation. This isn't a deductible offense, but it does eliminate any symmetrical anomaly that might make the judge look closer as well as demonstrating keen attention to detail. The seats should be closely inspected for every detail where dirt can build up. I have seen beautiful vehicles with more money invested in them than my house which had dirt between the seats that was easily seen when viewed from the proper angle. Even though it was overlooked, it could have easily been remedied if the time was taken to look for problems with a fresh set of eyes as well as

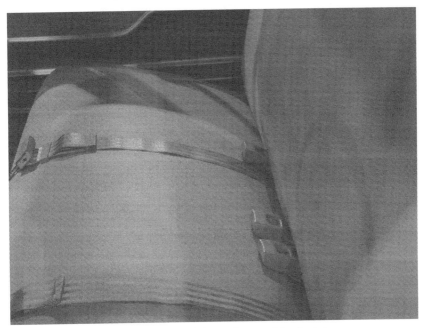

Illustration 5: Seat belts are straight and posed for judging.

from all angles.

Here is a technique that will help make your interior stand out relating to the seat belts. The seat belts should be positioned, or posed, and not left strewn about as if having been removed from the last drive. Some vehicles have clips that are mounted to the

Prepare To Be Judged

front of the seat that the belts can be attached to when not in use. If you don't have these, at least adjust the belts so they are straight and equal in length. This can also be done where all the belts in the vehicle are lined up except the drivers belt. This belt is positioned something like a folded down sheet on a freshly made bed. This can give the impression of being invited in for a drive. The belts should be clean and closely detailed. This

Illustration 6: The wheel is matched to the gauges and the rest of the interior as well as being indexed.

includes any stains, dust, and grime that has built up over the years. Seat belts are another item that are often overlooked.

The instrument panel should be spotless and have no dust accumulation. All corners and crevices should be detailed to a new condition. All knobs and switches should be oriented in the same direction to display that posed look. The steering wheel should be straight. This is of course dependent on whether or not the vehicle is displayed with its wheels straight. The dash and steering wheel will also be judged for quality such as scratches on the gauges or cracks in the steering wheel. The steering wheel should be detailed well to remove all fingerprints and built

Interior

up grime. Keep in mind that the steering wheel is the primary interface between you and your vehicle. It is what you use to hang on, control, feel the road, and finesse through the corners. Be sure to give it the attention that it deserves for the function it performs.

Dash / Console

Clean the dash all the way up where it is most difficult nearest the glass. Be sure to clean all the corners. If various elements of the interior are painted, look closely for scratches and chips and repair as necessary. Any scratches in the instrument cluster should be repaired. The glove box should be aligned with the rest of the trim on the dash. Any chrome or polished surface should be bright and clean. You will be deducted points for any pitted or checked surfaces.

If the dash and console are custom made, there should be a flow and good design that fits with the overall theme of the vehicle. This is a subjective point of view but if you're at the point of fabrication, think about the details. In some shows, you may be required to demonstrate that all the features of the vehicle function correctly. Be prepared for this. It is wise to determine the requirements prior to the day of the show. Any console compartment covers should be aligned with the rest of the trim on the console. If the vehicle has a manual transmission, the shifter boot should be well detailed as the dirt can easily be missed within the deep crevices.

Instrumentation and Electrical

Interior wiring should not be visible on most everything except race vehicles and even then, it can be hidden. If it is visible, it should be routed cleanly and be very well organized. Hanging or drooping wires are a dead giveaway that details are not being addressed. It is an extremely easy fix to help the vehicle present better. As far as the instrumentation goes, all the gauges should be clean and mounted correctly. They should be straight and aligned with each other. The rule isn't hard and fast, an exception to this might be in a race vehicle where the tachometer is oriented so the red line is mounted straight up and easy to read during competition.

The lettering on the instruments and the instruments themselves should be consistent. Using more than one manufacturer of gauges or having different styles intermixed could be considered bad form. If the lettering or colors are faded on the instruments, this is not necessarily a deductible item. If they are in otherwise good condition, there is some latitude for vehicles that are old. To fully restore the instruments you may need to have the faces re-screened to regain the full splendor of the original look. With customized vehicles, having the instruments match the theme of the vehicle is very important since poorly chosen design will stand out in a negative way.

Illustration 7: Many hours were spent on this neat and clean wiring job. For aesthetics, shrink wrap may have looked better than crimp-on connectors.

Wiring that is seen between the main body and the door should be appropriately covered and protected such as with split loom tubing and rubber grommets. Hanging wires through two drilled

Interior

holes won't cut it though it may cut the wire. Many times this won't be seen if the doors aren't open, but it is yet another detail to maintain.

Floor Covering

The floor coverings should be a well understood and easily detailed item of the interior since they take the majority of abuse inside a vehicle. Floor coverings range widely in the types that are available. Wood floors, rubber mats, carpets, and carpeted mats are among the varieties. The first detail a judge looks for is cleanliness. Whatever type of floor covering you have, it should look new or as new as possible. Carpets should be vacuumed so there is absolutely no foreign material visible. All uncarpeted vehicles should have any indication of being driven removed from harder surfaces such as mats, vinyl flooring, or the hard rubber or plastic inserts in the carpet at the drivers position. A final wipe down or vacuum should be done while performing the last details when setting up the vehicle at the show. Pay attention to areas that may be difficult to see such as under the dashboard and under the seats. The judges will likely have a flashlight and closely scrutinize all the locations they can see. Any little dirt will count against your score.

The next aspect is the quality of materials and any visible wear in the coverings. The high traffic wear areas are especially noticeable on the floor under the driver. An individual driver will tend to rest their feet in the same location which causes significant wear even with little movement. You might want to get a set of mats for driving to protect the coverings themselves that can be removed prior to show. If the vehicle is designed to have mats or are required by design or factory finish, an extra set that is normally unused would be a good replacement for show purposes. Keep in mind that dirt will accumulate under mats as well that can still cause wear and damage to the floor coverings. If the vehicle either came with or is designed to have floor mats, they should be positioned correctly in the passenger compartment. After miles of driving, mats will shift depending

Prepare To Be Judged

on how the driver and passengers position their feet. Prior to judging, you'll want to position the mats so they are straight and correctly located.

Other locations to watch for are the edges of the coverings such as up near the firewall and under the dash. The coverings should fit well and be in place and not flopping down. On some models, various features protrude through the coverings such as a headlight dimmer switch or seat belts. Holes such as these should have quality edging and not be ragged.

Trim and Bright Work

The bright work that is in the interior includes all the other highlights such as door handles, window cranks, mirror adjusters, power window switches, ash trays, cigarette lighters (not in the dashboard), and any other feature that may traditionally be chromed. On later vehicles, many of these items are not bright

Illustration 8: Even though this door panel is of extremely high quality, the window cranks could have been aligned to match the door handle.

anymore; however these features will still be scrutinized. Judging of these features is based on quality such as the finish and cleanliness. Many such items have finely detailed design features that can trap dirt or be worn from use so a replacement or repair may be in order.

Aside from quality of these items, there are adjustments that can be made for presentation purposes that may enhance your standing, most of which relate to the window cranks. This isn't applicable for vehicles with power windows or without window adjusters of any kind. There are a set number of turns to roll a window up or down and the crank itself should always be in the same ending position when the window is all the way up or down. If the window is all the way down, remove the crank handle and position it pointing directly down. I've seen vehicles where the crank is positioned at the bottom of the turn when the window is down, and positioned at the top when the window is up.

All vehicles have some variation in this respect so do some testing with yours. Be sure to position all of the cranks in the same direction. Pointing the crank directly down isn't required as you may have other design effects that you want to convey. I have seen window cranks positioned in the same orientation as the door handle which has a pleasing effect. Mainly, you want to avoid the cranks looking as if they were installed without thought and positioned at some random point on the circle where all the cranks in the vehicle are mis-matched.

Trunk / Bed

The trunk of a car (boot in Britain) or bed of a truck are traditionally the most utilitarian part of a vehicle. Prior to restoration, these receive the least amount of attention since they perform the most menial task of hauling stuff. As stated before, if the judges can't see it, it doesn't exist, good or bad. If the trunk is closed, there are no points awarded. The trunk is a compartment that is fairly simple to present well. A simple cleaning will at least earn some points. Make sure the jam surrounding the

Prepare To Be Judged

opening is spotless including the weather stripping. Empty the compartment of all items that aren't part of the display such as cleaning supplies, spare parts, or other miscellaneous items.

Illustration 9: Extremely clean and well presented stock appearing trunk.

An addition of carpet is a nice touch or simply a factory mat. Think of the trunk as yet another interior compartment and one that, aside from the discomfort, anyone would like to be in. Some elements of the trunk that should also be considered are the jack, spare tire, remote battery installation, custom fuel cell, or nitrous bottle. All of these items should be highly detailed, installed in a clean and orderly manner, and viewed with a critical eye toward presentation.

One last item relating to the trunk also relates to the vehicle bodywork. From inside the trunk of many vehicles, the body panels can be seen which may give an indication of the quality of bodywork. Panel replacements with lower quality welding or body filler oozing through filled holes will not be viewed

Interior

Illustration 10: Another clean and well presented custom trunk. Note the panels covering the inside of the fender.

well and may indicate the detail of other parts of the vehicle. If you have the option of customizing a vehicle, depending on the class entered, and have blemishes like these, you may consider installing customized panels in the trunk to cover what you don't want seen. The trunk can be as simple as factory stock or highly

Illustration 11: This bed has been refinished beautifully and displays as well as the rest of the truck.

Prepare To Be Judged

customized to match the theme of a custom ride, but as in all details of the vehicle, it should be appealing to view, organized, and perfectly clean.

The bed of a truck is another utilitarian component of a vehicle. As with a trunk, all elements that aren't part of your display should be removed. The bed should be perfectly clean in all corners and crevices. Depending on the age of the vehicle, the construction of the bed may be wood or steel. A steel bed will be simply a matter of detailing but if you're at the bodywork stage, spending the extra time to get the walls and floor of the bed straight will pay off.

Illustration 12: Not only was the bed refinished, but an excellent customized access panel was installed to hide the fuel filler.

The bed should have equivalent bodywork as the exterior of the vehicle. With a bed constructed of wood, the boards can be removed and refinished. This effort is well worth the time and the expense is relatively low. Finishing the wood to a furniture grade quality really stands out. The hardware that retains all the wood should at least be detailed. Another option is to replace the hardware with stainless steel or chrome pieces which nicely set

Interior

off the new wood finish of the floor.

An extra touch might be to have the hardware elements chromed to a high sheen. An added detail that can add points and improve the overall look is custom side rails that fit into the dunnage pockets of the bed. For beds of all kinds, the hardware should be highly detailed. This includes the latches, hinges, chains, and any other hardware relating to the bed.

Convertible Top

Having a topless vehicle is a wonderful thing. It not only increases the value of the vehicle in most cases, it gives a sense of freedom while driving when the top is dropped. Unfortunately, when the top is down, the scoring applies as in other categories where if the judge can't see it, they can't score it. This means that the top should be up even though the vehicle probably shows better when it is retracted. One possible workaround for this is to partially drop the top but leaving it up enough so the judges can see it all. This is not only a technique that allows the judges to score the top, it also may be seen to improve the presentation of the vehicle as a whole. With the top partially down, it is as if the top were in motion and being put down for an evening cruise. Showing the top in this way also gives the judges the ability to see all the latch mechanisms and that the top functions correctly.

From the quality aspect of the top, the judges will look at the quality of the material, all the seams, interior padding or structural elements, and rear window. All of these should present as if the top were new. Any hardware or structural element will be inspected for quality of finish. If the top is in poor condition such as with a hazy rear window or discolored material or some other defect, you may want to consider putting the top down and not have it detract from the rest of the vehicle. You may still receive some points for being a convertible, but that is dependent on the show and judge.

Prepare To Be Judged

Engine

The engine can be considered the heart of your vehicle not only because it is the pump that allows the vehicle to move, it is also one of the key features that show goers will want to see. Spectators want to see what generates all the raw power and the exhaust note that transforms your vehicle from a simple commuter into a historic and artistic creation. In terms of judging, the engine is also a major component of your vehicle that makes it shine or highly detracts from the overall view. Fortunately, the engine can be readied for show without too much investment from your wallet. What the task forgoes in expense, it makes up for with labor.

With all the various chemicals coursing through its veins and sometimes seeping out, exposure to exterior elements and a multitude of locations for dirt and grime to collect, the engine can be tedious and labor intensive to maintain show quality. The effort, however, will pay off if you spend the time to fully detail the engine to showroom condition whether that be stock or modified.

Authenticity

Depending on the type of vehicle that you have and which class you've entered, you may be bound by various restrictions. A factory stock vehicle should be equipped as though it were new

Illustration 1: This engine has an excellent appearance within its bay. The color and bright work are consistent with the rest of the vehicle.

or possibly could have been when new. The goal is to be as authentic to the type of vehicle as possible in keeping with the theme of the build. This applies to all classes, not just factory stock. Vintage rods or what you might call rat rods won't have much in the way of new and shiny accessories since that detracts from the theme. Pro-Street vehicles will have a lot of chrome and paint on their obscenely (in a good way) large motors. In all of these cases the engine should fit the build.

One way to increase the perceived quality of the vehicle is

Engine

Illustration 2: Notice the inconsistency of the hose clamps on this otherwise well detailed engine.

to add any factory equipment or options that were originally available for the make and model of your vehicle but weren't included on your particular car. This is generally limited to stock classes but the same idea applies to modified classes. Adding air conditioning to a stock vehicle is a valid modification provided the option was originally available for that car. Doing so will retain the stock appearance as well as add to the feature list of the vehicle. For modified classes, adding air conditioning whether it was originally available or not is worth points because of the modification to the original vehicle not because of the added feature. Air conditioning is just an example. Other items might include special induction systems, exhaust features, suspension upgrades, and power brakes or steering.

Another aspect relating to authenticity is a bit more removed. No matter what type of vehicle you're building, there are those

Prepare To Be Judged

who hold to the idea that the make of engine should match the make of the vehicle. They generally regard a GM vehicle with a Ford engine as something of a lower class citizen. This probably shouldn't be deducted in many classes other than stock, but it is possible that a judge's feelings may come out a bit. I do understand some of the reasoning for this type of build and don't recommend building a vehicle for anyone's taste but your own, but it is something to keep in mind. The decisions of the type of engine to install is made long before any show and is getting a bit out of scope for this topic.

The last item relating to authenticity of the engine relates to all the various bits that make it more than just a big lump of iron or aluminum. This includes the belts, hoses, hose clamps, battery, and wiring connectors. These are the smaller detail items that should fit with the vehicle theme. One example is to have all the same type of hose clamps. This may be either the factory style spring tensioned clamps, threaded band clamps, or ultra-modern billet clamps. Also be sure to use the correct size clamps. A threaded band clamp that has been tightened down to secure a hose with a long tail hanging out is a sure sign that you used whatever you could find and not the properly sized unit. The specific type you use isn't as important as keeping them consistent and authentic to the build.

A vehicle with a variety of parts that don't fit the theme, don't fit properly, or simply look like they've been put together out of whatever was available at the time of assembly shows a lack of attention to detail. This is a game of focus and attention and those with the most of both will not only perform well with the judges, they will have a product that they can be proud of for their own enjoyment.

Wiring

The wiring on a vehicle is generally most visible in the engine compartment. Typical wiring elements include spark plugs, battery, coil, lighting, and horn, as well as many others. While the engine compartment is the predominant area of visible wiring, it

Engine

Illustration 3: Very little wiring is visible on this engine, but what is visible is neatly organized.

can also be seen in other locations such as on the chassis or in the trunk. There are a number of concepts and techniques discussed here to improve the quality of your wiring and help your vehicle be viewed favorably by the judges.

First, if the wiring is not meant to be seen, it shouldn't be seen. This may seem obvious but I have judged a number of vehicles with wires hanging from under the dash or chassis and dragging on the ground. This lack of attention to detail will not go well with the judges.

For more customized vehicles, hiding the wires that are traditionally viewable is a common technique. This gives the vehicle a very clean and uncluttered appearance and highlights the features that are intended to be seen. Hiding the wiring also promotes a sense of mystery for the viewer in that they have to look hard to discover the routing. For the judges, performing this technique well may generate more points as the level of difficulty is increased. Remember that the judges inspect every inch of your vehicle with flashlights and mirrors. The casual observer may not see that the hidden wiring is unceremoniously stuffed into some less obvious compartment, but the judge might. The execution of the technique is as important as the technique itself.

For the wiring that is intended to be visible, it should be routed in as clean a fashion as possible. This may take the form of making 90° bends for every angle and securing it appropriately or creating guides that gently curve the wire through the intended route. The possibilities are endless and aren't necessarily important, but the wiring should look like a purposeful installation and not like a jumble of spaghetti or routed as the crow flies with no regard to proper containment. The judges will recognize that special care has been taken in installation and preparation of the wiring.

The last detail concerning the wiring is its general appearance. This is separate from the way it is installed. The appearance includes the quality of the connections, the types of connectors, the cleanliness of the wiring, the specific covering of the harnesses, and potentially the correctness of the wiring itself in terms of originality.

When using add-on connectors for your wiring, at a minimum they should be consistent across all the wiring in the vehicle. A mixed variety of connectors including stock, performance and the cheap crimp-on style is not attractive and will likely lose you some points. Keeping the connections consistent shows forethought and attention to detail. I do recommend staying away from replacing all the connectors with the crimp-on style. While they are simple to install, they don't provide the best connections and give the appearance of a low quality build. Wires should be connected appropriately to their components. Twisted ends held together with electrical tape won't go over well with the judges. Soldering connections and covering with shrink wrap will provide a much better performing connection as well as appear more professional.

The type of wire will also be scrutinized. As with the connectors,

Engine

Illustration 4: Even though the wiring on this rat rod is very utilitarian, it is still routed cleanly.

keeping the wiring consistent throughout the whole vehicle is important. With customized vehicles, wiring that was either left in a stock state or replaced with stock wiring should be matched with wiring that has a more stock appearance. If the vehicle has harnesses that have obviously been replaced or purpose built, pairing those with stock harnesses won't appear consistent and may give the impression that the stock appearing harness had been ignored in the build and left as-is. The same is also true when you have a stock vehicle with custom made harnesses. The new ones will appear out of place with the old and points will be deducted.

There are a number of variations of coverings for wiring harnesses including corrugated plastic tubing, shrink wrap, or simply wrapped with various types of cloth or plastic tape. Keep the coverings consistent with the rest of the vehicle and appropriate to the design that you're intending to portray along with cleaning or replacing imperfect or damaged portions.

Plumbing

Much like the electrical elements in the engine compartment, the plumbing components need to be chosen, detailed, and routed with care. There are a few types of plumbing that you'll have to deal with in the engine compartment. They include heating, cooling, oil lines, fuel lines, brake lines and possibly others such as nitrous or water injection.

When choosing these elements it is most important to pick the proper materials that are consistent with the rest of the build. If you are working on a factory stock vehicle then original equipment and factory marked hoses are in order. On the other end of this spectrum are stainless covered hoses with highly polished billet ends. No matter the case, the hoses should be clean and routed appropriately. A careless mix of hose types or poor installation will show a lack of detail.

Hard plumbing such as fuel, brake and some cooling lines, a key detail is in how they are routed. Multiple lines should be run parallel with each other and make purposeful bends for aesthetic purposes. The lines shouldn't look like they were installed purely to get the vehicle on the road. Take the time to do the job well and make it look good.

Engine

Plating and Bright Work

The bright coatings on engine components can range widely and are key to highlighting aspects of an engine compartment. Some owners have chosen to implement large amounts of chrome while others retain factory stock appearances where the brightest parts are simply a gloss black. Traditionally, these are elements that have some type of bright appearance though later model vehicles have been built with much less bright materials due to production expense. This should be accounted for in the stock classes but modified vehicles will benefit from re-coating or replacing parts with ones that have more appeal. Examples of coatings include chrome, stainless, bare metal, brushed or polished aluminum, and anodized materials.

Illustration 5: This engine has significant amounts of bright elements that show well under the bright lights. Notice the clip-on light that highlights the engine compartment features.

Both stock and modified classes will benefit from bright work elements, but the customized vehicles will have the advantage and freedom to add as many as the builder desires. The key to these elements is their quality and detail. High quality finishes will not be scored well if they are not detailed properly, but the opposite is not quite as true. Lower quality finishes that

Prepare To Be Judged

are detailed to a high degree will likely not only be judged less harshly, but will display better and brighter.

Detail

The engine compartment, while not necessarily a physically large part of the vehicle has a considerably high amount of detail. With all the parts and pieces, wires and hoses, linkage and containers, and brackets and mounts, there are an untold amount of places that need to be cleaned and adjusted for detail. Since this is the case, the category for detail may be a separate item considered by the judges. Special attention should be given to this area. Winners take many hours preparing the overall compartment verifying that nothing is missed. This process shouldn't be rushed and you should check your work and possibly have others do the same. The judges will be using a flashlight which will also be useful for your own preparation and validation. The main advantage here is

Illustration 6: This engine compartment has a number of different finishes and is well detailed.

Engine

that the process is generally low cost. Even though the price may be low, the cost in time and labor make up for it.

During the detailing process, be sure to touch up any chips or missing paint as well as clean everything that can possibly be seen. The cleanup may only be a simple dusting but I've seen dust on the engine cradle determine whether the vehicle took first or second place in its class.

Paint that was originally sprayed such as on the engine block is challenging to touch up since you may have to remove a lot of parts for access to tape off difficult components. A simple technique that will sometimes work is to spray some of the matching paint into a small container and use a brush for application. This eliminates the majority of the problems you face by having to re-spray particularly troublesome locations.

Installation and Engineering

The installation category is one that would typically be applied to more customized vehicles. In most cases, stock type installations won't really have much to be judged as long as they are installed correctly with parts that are in good and clean condition. For the customs, the thought process for judging the category is to view the engineering behind the engine installation. What special techniques were used or simply the quality of work that was employed. In many cases, the high amount of parts and pieces present in more stock vehicles are hidden in custom vehicles. Since customized vehicles have a more clean appearance, the detail that is present will likely be scrutinized more closely.

Firewall / Engine Bay

On many vehicles, the firewall and engine compartment is more than just a place for the vehicle plumbing and electrical services to pass. They are a backdrop or frame to focus your attention on the engine. There is a lot of opportunity for detail here and unfortunately it can be a lot of work and can be quite time consuming since there are so many parts, wires, and hoses

Prepare To Be Judged

Illustration 7: Nicely customized firewall detail shown here.

Engine

to work around. Because of these difficulties, many show participants won't fully prepare their engine compartment to its fullest.

To really maximize the engine bay, an extreme detailed cleaning is in order. Even when the finish isn't perfectly shiny or has blemishes, an extremely clean engine bay will be noticed because the owner made that extra effort of time and work to maximize impact. This may include removing all components from the engine bay such as wiring, hoses, electrical components, or structural members to be able to fully access where it is difficult or impossible to reach but still visible. Some will even remove the engine to gain access to all those hard to reach areas and have the ability to detail the engine itself without hindrance. Beyond the simple cleaning, though it really isn't that simple, is the next step in preparing the engine compartment and maximizing the finished appearance by removing and repairing any blemishes and applying the proper original or customized paint schemes.

Many vehicle engine compartments, especially newer ones, simply have a semi-flat black finish that should be free of blemishes and be cleaned wherever visible. This type of engine bay has such a seemingly simple appearance, but many vehicles have more than a simple semi-flat black paint. I have seen engine compartments that have upwards of five or six different tones and textures of black. It's a mistake to compete in a stock class with a vehicle like this if you don't take care to get all the finishes correct.

Other more customized vehicles or some stock manufacturers finish their engine bays with paint to match the body. Once again the engine bay should be clean wherever visible and the paint should be nearly as shiny as the exterior body. The body and paint-work here generally isn't expected to be the quality of the external body, but once again, details win races and the further you go, the more reward.

Some highly customized vehicles have gone that extra step and fully replaced the firewall and inner fenders either for engineering necessity or aesthetics. If a larger engine or exhaust are installed and won't fit within the factory body panels, some modification is performed. Some vehicles have a very clean and high tech look and replace these panels with very simple, clean, and body matched painted panels in keeping with the theme of the overall vehicle. In all of these cases, the customizations are a large undertaking and should be performed well. The quality of any visible welding should be high. Bashing a panel with a hammer or cutting it away with a 'blue tip wrench' to fit that high flow exhaust will not garner any points and will show that the modifications were not planned nor executed per a design.

Once again, many of these design decisions aren't ones that are performed right before a show, they are made when the vehicle is being fabricated and built. If you're at this point, take the extra time and plan out a design that not only functions properly, but looks good too. Cleverly engineered routes and placement of plumbing and electrical elements shows forethought and detailed thinking. Likewise, a clean, flat, customized firewall will look good; however, adding another element such as a design characteristic like a body line formed into the steel to match the overall theme ties the normally flat panel to the rest of the vehicle. There are very few vehicles with parts that are purely straight and flat without any design elements in them. Embossing some type of design into the firewall helps it stand out among the rest.

Chassis

The underside of a vehicle is often the last place that receives attention mainly because it is not only difficult to see from a spectator's perspective, but is more difficult to truly prepare for show. The chassis is very time consuming to maintain at a high level because of all the road grime and debris.

As far as show vehicle chassis are concerned, we can break them down into about three categories. The first is the purpose built show vehicle that is highly detailed from stem to stern and top to bottom. Those vehicles don't usually see very much road time but every aspect of the chassis must be inspected since the painted, chromed and other finishes are of such high quality. The second category includes vehicles that have generally stock appearing or mild custom work performed on the underside of the vehicle. These vehicles are probably driven regularly or semi-regularly and kept free of major fluid leaks and grime. The last category includes vehicles with little or no attention paid to the underside except for general maintenance or repair when necessary and have a chassis that appears no different than any other typical daily driven vehicle.

On the positive side of this difficult to maintain part of the vehicle, there are many folks who neglect the underside of their vehicle. This is potentially beneficial in a couple of ways. Since others aren't paying close attention to the less obvious parts, you may be able to score some points and widen the gap between you and them. The other aspect is that the judges may try to give some credit for any attempted preparation and won't be too harsh on the scoring when compared to the rest of the class being judged.

As competition gets tighter, more and more focus on detail is required to get on the podium. In the professional show car classes, the underside of the vehicle receives as much attention as the top. The parts and pieces of the chassis are painted, plated, prepped, and polished all to push the limits of automotive artwork.

Wheels / Tires (Detailed / Indexed)

As most enthusiasts know, the wheels and tires on a vehicle set the tone of the whole image and can make or break it. While the choice of vehicle 'shoes' is a personal one, this is an easy place to gain some points. First of all, the wheels and tires should be cleaned and detailed to a spotless condition. This includes removing the wheels from the vehicle and cleaning the back side as if it were the front of the wheel.

The tires should be a matched set. The brand and model of tire should not vary from one wheel to the next. Of course there may be differences in size, but that is acceptable. Sometimes this can be problematic when a vehicle doesn't get many miles put on it. The tires can last a long time and it is possible that if a replacement is required, the particular model is no longer available and becomes much more difficult to match.

The condition and cleanliness of any hardware such as lug nuts or bolts and knock-offs, hubcaps, and wheel covers should also

Chassis

Illustration 1: All the wheels on this truck were positioned with the valve stem in this location. Also, the manufacturers emblem is oriented level with the ground.

be scrutinized and appropriately addressed. This also includes the back side and tread of the tire. Ideally, the the tires will look as new as if they were newly installed. Some folks will put tire dressing on the sidewall of the tires to really make them shine. This is a personal judgment call. Tires with dressing will stand out and have a nice appearance. I personally don't care for that look but wouldn't score lower because of it. I'm looking for quality, not only what I like. Normal tire wear isn't generally an issue as long as there aren't odd wear patterns. Bald tires are not acceptable. As a general rule, the newer the tires, the better they will appear. This may also be a good time to make any touch up or repair to painted alloy or steel wheels. Minor repairs such as these are not difficult to perform and will remove any obvious blemishes. White walls should be bright white with no curb marks on the sidewall.

Prepare To Be Judged

Illustration 2: Not only is the wheel alligned with the center cap horizontal and readable, the tire is also indexed with the wheel.

The second technique is to index the tires and wheels. This is by far the most overlooked and possibly least known items that the judges score and it is very simple and inexpensive to correct and can set a vehicle apart from the rest in its class. This technique is not only scored at judged events, it is widely used in automotive photography. This goes back to the idea that when presenting your vehicle to be judged, you are setting a pose that highlights the way the vehicle looks. Indexing is an easy way to add points to your score and there are very few vehicles I've seen being judged over the last few years that have had this done.

What indexing means is that you index or align the tires and wheels so they all have the same orientation. There are two elements to this technique as the tires and wheels are indexed separately. The tires are indexed when they are mounted to the wheels. All tires should be oriented in the same direction with

Chassis

relation to the valve stem and some identifying mark on the tire. The identifying mark could be the space between words on the tire, an embossed emblem, or any other distinguishing mark. Some tire shops do this as a matter of policy when mounting tires but most don't. The advantage to this technique is that it doesn't cost any more and doesn't take any more time than simply mounting a tire wherever it may land.

Indexing the wheels, as with the tires, is aligning them so they all have the same orientation with each other. This will likely require the use of a jack at the show to slightly lift each corner of the vehicle and rotate the wheel to match the rest. Personally, I like having the valve stem directly at the bottom of the wheel with the tire brand oriented at the center and at the top but you should consider how this will line up with any other accessories. The wheel alignment also extends to any hub caps, wheel covers, and knock offs. Having the orientation of all these elements the same shows attention to detail and poses your vehicle to show its best.

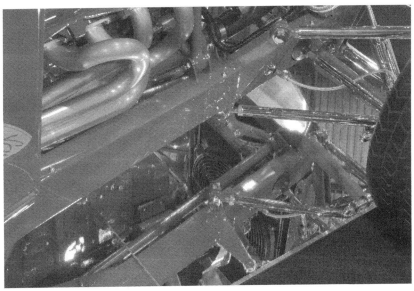

Illustration 3: The use of mirrors allows the judges to easily view the chassis and suspension.

Suspension, Steering / Brakes, Rear-end

The next stage of the chassis includes what is next most visible. The steering linkage, brake hardware, rear-end and suspension components are easily seen by simply changing your view a bit to a lower point. Some brake hardware can nearly be inspected by looking through the spaces in some wheel designs. Ensuring all these components are clean and in good condition makes a good impression. Be sure to pull out a flashlight and mirror and view all components from every angle as it is very easy to miss grime by only looking from the most common perspective. This is the way the judges inspect the vehicle especially when the competition is tight.

The more a vehicle is driven, the more difficult it is to maintain show quality and the more hours that will have to be invested to get the proper result. Use your fingers or possibly gloves to inspect those hard to see areas where the dirt may be hiding. All of these parts and pieces and their finishes should be in as-new condition. Any visible grayish brown road grime will be reflected in the score.

Frame and the Rest of the Underside

The remaining part of the chassis left to be judged includes the frame, floor pans, exhaust system, drive line, fuel and brake lines and any other elements found under a vehicle. The underside of

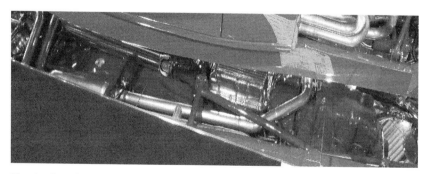

Illustration 4: All the underside components can be easily viewed on this car. The time and effort to get to this level is readily apparent.

Chassis

the vehicle is generally judged fairly quickly in most classes for a number of reasons. Many of these vehicles are driven regularly and there isn't much to see that isn't expected on the underside of a daily driven vehicle. The bottom side many times hasn't received much, if any, attention which is readily visible and makes it unnecessary to closely scrutinize every aspect.

Illustration 5: Brake hardware can sometimes be viewed through the wheel.

In some cases, there isn't much to see under a vehicle because it is very low such as in low-rider or high performance super car classes. These vehicles are not only very low but are constructed in such a way to improve aerodynamics for high speed driving and there simply isn't anything to see. This can make the job of the judge more difficult but in the end, the judges can only score what they can see. If you want your highly detailed chassis on your extremely low vehicle judged fairly and to your benefit, make appropriate adjustments to your display such as putting the vehicle on stands or using mirrors.

For the high end show-only vehicles, the job is much more involved as all aspects need to be inspected because the vehicle is of extremely high quality from all points of view. With these

Prepare To Be Judged

close, and highly competitive contests, the judges may not only visually inspect the vehicle but they may use their fingers to feel above and inside the frame rails or anywhere else that is not readily visible to determine where the paint stops or rough edges are located. There tend to not be a large number of extremely customized vehicles in any given show due to their rarity and expense. This allows the judges to spend more time on each vehicle to closely examine all of its aspects. It is likely that they will spend a significant amount of time on their backs with flashlights and mirrors to inspect the vehicle from everywhere they can see and possibly feel. Since the judge is going to this effort, you should spend at least the same amount of time with your own inspection looking for the same types of flaws, blemishes, or simply dirt.

Illustration 6: This stock class vehicle demonstrates the great care and attention to detail.

From the judge's point of view, there should be no obvious signs of wear such as holes in the exhaust, loose or rubbing parts, leaking seals and the like. All visible parts should be clean and appear new with a uniform finish. Wires, fuel, and brake lines should be neatly routed and cleanly held in place. The

Chassis

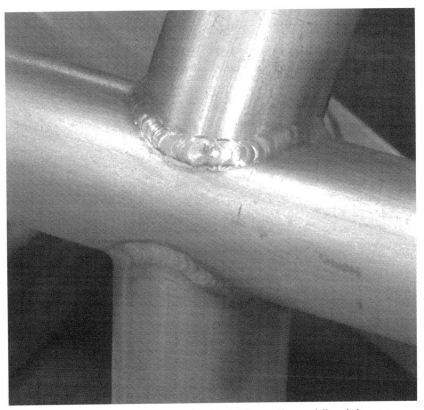

Illustration 7: This is one example of a high quality welding job on a bare metal tube frame.

underside of the body shouldn't have any dents or show signs of damage. The drive line, if applicable, should be clean and have a uniform finish. The frame should be clean and straight with no obvious rust or or structural defects. A custom frame should be constructed with clean and smooth welds as well as a good finish. As with the rest of the vehicle, whether it is stock or highly customized, the ideal is that the vehicle looks new and professional in terms of quality of workmanship and components.

Once I judged a vehicle that looked good at first glance; however, when I got under it I saw loose wires hanging down nearly to the ground by the engine and a puddle of oil collecting on the floor. Making the simple repairs to eliminate obvious flaws helps because the judge won't assume that the same lack of care was taken throughout the rest of the vehicle. In this case, if the owner

Prepare To Be Judged

had taken a few minutes to shove the wires out of site and stuff a rag up to block the oil, the general perception of the vehicle would have been much higher. Even though this wouldn't be the correct fix, it would be much better than leaving the obvious flaws alone. Take the time to attend to the simple repairs and detail items.

Presentation

Now that you've cleaned, detailed, fixed, adjusted, tweaked and massaged your vehicle so that it shines bright and stands out among all the rest, there is still one thing left when preparing for a show. You need to present the vehicle in a way that not only highlights the vehicle, but focuses the judges and spectators at your vehicle and its best attributes. This is like getting ready for a job interview. You may be the best candidate, but you have to convey that to the interviewer. You are trying to present yourself in the best light by showing up on time, being dressed appropriately, and being prepared to answer questions in the best way you know how. Although the techniques are different, the same is true when presenting your vehicle to those walking through a cruise-in or more importantly, the show judges who will be closely inspecting your vehicle.

There are a number of methods discussed here that may not push you to the top of the competition, but as with all the aspects of preparation, focusing on the details and maximizing all the assets you have will help. Not all of these methods will apply to

Prepare To Be Judged

Illustration 1: This display is highly detailed and is more elaborate than most. These vehicles would be very difficult to judge due to all the props. This was not an issue since they were for display only.

all shows and you'll need to determine what is appropriate for the show you're attending. A local cruise-in or club get-together will likely be much less formal than a full weekend show held at a convention center with an official judging staff. Do what is necessary but keep it fun, that's the reason we love this hobby.

Judge's Book

Your judge's book is a collection of your vehicle's history and details. It is the place where you put all your vehicle's pictures and history. This may include the build process, special historical documentation such as famous previous owners, magazine articles, or racing history. It is also where you should document particular options and innovations, especially difficult techniques or customizations which may not be readily obvious to the judges. Always err on the side of caution and include more. The book can be the determining factor if there are questions about

Presentation

Illustration 2: A typical judge's book demonstrating the history of the vehicle.

the authenticity of specific features that the judges may not know or design techniques that aren't readily apparent.

When putting together your judge's book, arrange the information and pictures by importance so the judge will see what is most amazing about your vehicle. Keep the information clear and include captions with the pictures so you have control of what is being communicated as well as giving the judges a specific message that you want them to know. Don't assume that the reader, or judge in this case, knows what you're thinking or trying to communicate.

The quality of the book may also garner some points but this shouldn't be the reason for winning an award. If you have a fully documented book with good pictures and presented well, there is a possibility, depending on the show, that you may earn some points for the effort. Currently in this information age, there are numerous on-line services that you can use to put together a one-of-a-kind book that is professionally bound and very reasonably priced. An effort like this will be rewarded. A simple photo album might get you on the board, but probably won't gain you the maximum score. Keep in mind that the vehicle should determine the win, not the book. This is also show and judge dependent. The overall premise is that the book be detailed and

Prepare To Be Judged

Illustration 3: The owner of this vehicle went a step further by continuing the vehicle theme onto the cover of the book.

of high quality and demonstrate that effort was taken.

One note of caution relating to the judge's book. Many vehicle owners love to fill their book with copious details of a particular part of the build such as the internals of the engine or body work. Those are important features and very interesting but try to keep a balanced approach and cover the vehicle as a whole. The problem with focusing too heavily on one area such as the engine is that the details can't be viewed. An approach like this will also leave other parts lacking. Cover the topic of your vehicle as a whole and bring to light all the pertinent details, not simply the ones in which you have a particular interest.

One last item related to the judge's book. When displaying your

Presentation

Illustration 4: A simple, high quality story board that flows with the display theme and effectively uses additional lighting.

vehicle, be sure to put the book in a location where the judge can find it. It would be a shame if you had a well constructed high quality book that the judge isn't able to locate.

Story Board

A story board is a common way, along with the judge's book, to convey a brief history of the vehicle with answers to some of the more common questions that you may receive. This is a good place to highlight details that the casual observer or judge may not know or see. Focus the attention of the viewer where you want it, on the positives. This is an advantage for non-scored events such as people's choice awards.

You can go too far with what you say though, I recommend staying positive. I've seen a board that gave the information in such a way that said "don't bother me with your stupid questions, I've heard them all before, this is all you need to know". Though not in those exact words, that was the essence. I suspect the

Prepare To Be Judged

Illustration 5: Very artistic and clever use of a body panel to tie the story board to the vehicle.

owner had been asked the same questions many times and was tired of answering. To me, the owner came across as being incredibly rude and if I were to judge that vehicle, it would give me a poor impression and I might want to be a bit more critical. Yes, judges are supposed to be objective, but the reality is that they are human.

The story board is an art display as well as informational and can be created in an infinite number of ways. You might include either current or historical photos whether that be of family history or something with more provenance such as race photos. You could include art along with the vehicle details. The sky is the limit here. Take the time to plan and execute the project well, it will be viewed and read by many people. If you're not very artistic, you may want to enlist the help of a vendor that provides the service of designing a personalized and professional looking display.

Story boards and informational displays have entered the information age and are being pushed to new heights. Flat panel

Presentation

displays with custom video presentations and kiosks have been employed to highlight already spectacular vehicles. No matter what is used, pay attention to the details so nothing detracts from the image you're intending to portray.

The judge's book, story board, or video display probably won't put you ahead of another vehicle that is better, but it is another element in presenting the vehicle well. If the competition is tight, these elements could put you over the top. The judges I've worked with wouldn't want to give an award to a lesser car simply on the merits of scored items that aren't directly part of the vehicle.

Illustration 6: An excellent display that ties the colors, textures and finishes together. The use of mirrors and wheel stands set this car up to be admired as if on a pedistal.

Participants Interview

One other possible way of getting specific information to the judges is through an actual conversation with them prior to judging. Any special engineering or design features should be communicated to the judge if possible. This can be done through the judge's book or direct communication during a judging session. Some shows may have a specified time for such a conversation but limit the length of such interviews so be prepared to point out the most special features of your vehicle that may not be obvious.

Illustration 7: The theme of this display highlights the color combination of the car. The wheel stands aid in viewing the chassis on an otherwise extremely low vehicle.

It is worth spending some time on preparing your message to the judges in advance. List all the customized, engineered, and design elements. Prioritize them in order of importance and be prepared to elaborate on each one in order. Give it your best shot even if you run out of time. If necessary, have some notes so you don't have to rely on your memory. To some folks, this type of conversation might be stressful as it is somewhat like an interview. This is a simple tip for keeping your message straight. Also, try to think of the interview as more of a friendly conversation between two gear-heads.

Presentation

Innovation, Concept & Execution

This is a category that may or may not be included in a scored event, but it is worth being prepared. The concept and execution category is fairly subjective and is where the judges are given latitude in awarding some points to a vehicle that may have a particularly interesting design or well thought out features that aren't covered elsewhere in the judging categories. A well documented judge's book may help here. Indicating the thought processes that went into design decisions will show that you've really thought through your creation. This category receives more weight in modified classes. Stock classes are not competitive in this area since they are limited to factory design.

Illustration 8: Excellent use of props that enhance the vehicle with themed paint.

Display

When putting your vehicle on display, keep in mind that you are striking a 'pose' and you want to put your best foot forward. Make an effort to help your vehicle stand out. Set up a scene that portrays your vehicle as the centerpiece such as at the drive-in (movies or burgers) or at a gas station. Some elements that can show off your vehicle are color matched floor coverings or stanchions with velour theater rope that matches or accents the color of your vehicle. Other elements might be specialized tool boxes, gas pumps, or fire extinguishers. These types of items show that you made that extra effort. Remember a display won't make your vehicle the best and this category may only be worth a few points, if any at all, so going overboard may be more work than it's worth. It gives you the potential of a few more points over a vehicle that has done nothing. Once again, it is about having fun and if you want to make a highly complex display with music, flashing lights, and animatronics, go for it. It will be enjoyed.

Illustration 9: Clever camouflage of a storage container for various items and what looks to be electrical infrastructure.

There are some effective techniques for displaying your vehicle such as mirrors directly on the floor or carefully positioned so the underside of the vehicle can easily be viewed. Think of the mirrors that are used in shoe stores, they are angled in such a way that you can easily see what your shoes look like from a

Presentation

standing position. The addition of lighting might be appropriate for especially dark regions that are difficult to see. Some paint will come alive with the proper lights. Covering a drab gray concrete floor with some type of floor covering can also highlight your vehicle. Use a color or design that either matches or complements your vehicle.

An excellent way of improving the view of a vehicle chassis and suspension is to put the tires on stands to raise the vehicle. This allows the passer by to more easily view under the vehicle. I've seen this done in a way where the vehicle was not only raised on stands but each stand was a different height so that the vehicle is displayed as if it were on a slope. Another similar method is to replace one of the stands with a specially made stand that not only holds the vehicle up, but replaces a wheel and bolts to the hub. This allows for especially good viewing of the suspension.

When displaying your vehicle, make sure that it is fully open and available to be judged. Opening the hood/bonnet, trunk/boot and at least one window. The vehicle may look better when the doors, hood and trunk are closed but if the judges can't see particular features, they won't be judged. Help the judges award you as many points as possible. Now, this is dependent on how an event is judged. In the shows that I have worked, the judges are not allowed to touch the vehicles so it is "what you see is what you get." If the trunk is closed, that category gets no points. In other events, the judges are allowed to run their hands all over the vehicle, especially in hidden locations to feel for imperfections. Be sure you know the requirements and judging criteria prior to the show.

If you have imperfections that you're trying to hide, carefully 'pose' the vehicle in such a way so that the issue isn't visible or at least isn't as obvious. I have seen this done where a seat belt was carefully covering a minor hole in a seat. Using this technique doesn't mean that a cardboard box of cleaning supplies should cover the rust hole in the trunk. However, a vintage tool box, part of your presentation that is 'displayed' while covering the rust hole in the trunk would be valid and may be effective.

Prepare To Be Judged

Try to be as subtle as possible here. A large stuffed animal in an odd place might cover the flaw, but without it being part of the theme you're trying to convey, it might stand out as odd and inspire the judges to look more closely than they may have otherwise.

Another reason you may want to hide an item may be that it is less aesthetically pleasing as opposed to simply being a flaw. I saw a vehicle at the Barrett-Jackson auction that had a small vintage Coke cooler in the trunk. The car was a '32 Ford highboy with an identical red to match the cooler. The interesting part was that the cooler was fake and simply covered the trunk mounted battery. It was a very clever trick that made the vehicle appear that much nicer and covered a drab and uninteresting vehicle necessity.

No matter how you display your vehicle or what type of props you use, keep in mind that the judges still have to be able to judge the vehicle. This means they need easy access to all aspects of the vehicle. Don't make it difficult for the judges to do their job. Having lots of props surrounding the vehicle may look good from a display perspective, but compete with your other priority of allowing the judge to easily maneuver around the vehicle. Maintain accessibility so the judges can view all aspects of your vehicle without tripping or knocking over your props and potentially causing damage. Another reason for not having too many props is that you want to highlight your vehicle, not hide it. Don't let the props, signs, trophies or other accessories overpower the display and detract from the goal of presenting your car.

Location

If you have any say in where your vehicle is placed, choose your spot carefully. As they say in the real estate business, "location, location, location". This is also true in shows, especially with people's choice awards. Try to find a spot that will be heavily traveled by most of the spectators. This is a way of highlighting your vehicle over the rest of the competition. Some possible

Presentation

ways of doing this are to determine where you think foot traffic will be heavy. If the event is outdoor and it is a hot and sunny day, a nice shady spot can give your viewers a brief rest where they may focus their attention on your vehicle. If there are foot traffic bottle necks at the event such as moving from field to field or building to building, pick a spot where the people can't avoid seeing your car. This might be in the center of view as they enter a building or field. Stay close to the center of the action. If you think of the show as a cluster of vehicles, people may tend to make the quick turn at the outskirts of the cluster and won't give as much attention to your vehicle as they might if you're located more centrally to the event.

Some locations that might be questionable are entrances, registration locations, vendor booths, and restrooms. While these locations will likely have heavy foot traffic, the traffic is focused on other items that are not necessarily vehicle related. The people will be looking and thinking of other things besides your vehicle. This isn't to say that these locations won't work. I have seen them go both ways, choosing one of these types of spots may just be a gamble.

One last decision in choosing a location is to think about what will be parked adjacent to your car. Consider the type of vehicle and its quality, flashiness, uniqueness, and color. Think about how your vehicle will stand out if you're in a row of all the same make and model. While it can look cool with a row of a particular make, it doesn't help your particular vehicle stand out. Also, what if you're in a row of vehicles that are all the same color as yours? Try to park next to contrasting colors that will help highlight your vehicle and not blend in with its neighbor. These situations don't make your vehicle stand out in the crowd. If you're parked next to an extremely flashy or particularly unique vehicle that you think may get a lot of attention, you may want to avoid that location even if they aren't in your class. The problem is that those vehicles may steal the attention away from your vehicle even if yours is of much higher quality. Ideally, you want your vehicle to be the memorable one in your section, on your row, and ultimately at the whole show.

Category Notes

Judges may have the ability to make notes about specific categories for both positive and negative reasons. These notes are mainly used in the event where questions arise as to why a specific category was scored in such a way. This will remind the judge of the particular element and vehicle and allow them to more clearly explain the score. This may dissuade the owner from potential complaints where they have determined their vehicle is better than what the judges thought.

On the positive note, this is a place where the judge can make note of a particularly high quality or innovative category. This is another area where the scale can be tipped but it isn't really something for which you can prepare. One possible use of this information is that there are sometimes special awards given. These can be given to vehicles that may not be the best overall, but have an especially high quality attribute such as the interior or paint. From what I've seen, events like to spread the awards around so a single vehicle won't steal the whole show. It makes for better drama.

How to Improve

Here we are at the end. Presumably, you've applied many, if not all, of the tips and techniques in this book to the best of your ability and have now competed. The question now is how to improve on those results. There is a big advantage in being in this position because now you're not the only one who has evaluated your car. Your car has been judged on a level playing field with others like it in its class.

In this chapter, we'll cover a number of ways to improve on what you've already accomplished for the next event. There is always room for improvement and there are very few perfect cars.

How is the Event Judged

In advance of the next event, find out how the cars are judged and learn the judge's criteria. You can contact the event promoter for this information. This may be as simple as a phone call to discuss their methods. Some larger events have web sites dedicated to their show that include posted guidelines. The guidelines may range from a single sheet of classes and their scoring method to a very specific rule book by which participants and judges must abide. These resources can be a wealth of knowledge. You may find information you would never have known otherwise and taking the extra effort may pay dividends later when competing against those who aren't as proactive.

When contacting the organizers of the event, you may also be able to contact one or more of the judges and find out some of the areas where they focus their attention. Many judges have their specific area of interest or pet peeve and having a friendly conversation may give you some ideas as well as areas to focus your attention.

Another question you might ask a judge or promoter is what are the biggest areas for improvement that they've seen in the past. When I've judged shows, it became clear pretty fast that many of the participants didn't know what the judges were looking for in several areas. That is the main reason this book was written.

You may also want to ask what time the judging starts and when the gates open. Having the schedule can help you know how early you should arrive to perform any last minute details such as a final cleaning. Arrive early enough to allow time for your car to cool sufficiently so you can perform engine compartment work without being burned. This of course assumes that it didn't arrive in a trailer. Luck favors the prepared.

Score Sheets

The judge's score sheet is the final say on how your car performs. The sheet also determines what specific categories are being judged and how they should be scored. There are a number of types of score sheets that are specific to their respective classes such as stock, modified, rod, race/performance or motorcycle. Many items will overlap, but there are some that are specific to their respective class.

If the show you're attending has an official score sheet, ask to get a blank copy in advance of the show. These sheets are probably not secret and many promoters will be able to get you a copy for your own purposes but this is no guarantee. I've included an example in the back of this book. Having a blank sheet allows you to perform your own assessment against what will be finally scored.

Not only should you try to get a blank score sheet but after the show has been judged, request that you get a copy of the finalized score sheet for your car. This will give you the actual data that you'll use for later improvements. You can see where you scored well and where you need to put some more effort. This seems to be a little known point and most participants never ask for their results.

Talk with the Judges

I've already mentioned having a discussion with the judges prior to the event. This is where you should talk with them after the event. More specifically, talk with the judge or judges who scored your car. They not only saw your car, but the others in the class and have an independent perspective. Many times they'll be happy to do this because they, like you, have a love of vehicles and would like everyone to do their best.

Have the judge walk through the score sheet with you explaining why they scored as they did. Have them answer any questions you might have where any perceived discrepancies lie. This isn't a time to complain since the judge is doing this as a courtesy. Ask them where you should focus your efforts and what you could improve on for the next time.

Evaluate Your Score

Evaluating your score assumes that you have attained a copy of your own score sheet. Now that you have it, go over it carefully and objectively evaluate it compared to what you know of the quality standard of your vehicle. This will give you a good breakdown of where you should focus your efforts for the next event.

Think of this like having a test in school. You now have the scored test back in your hands and are allowed to retake the exam multiple times and the questions aren't changed. Unfortunately the analogy breaks down because an exam is easy to adjust to get the proper answers, whereas fixing some problems to improve scoring in the real world may take many hours of labor and potentially a lot of money.

Second Set of Eyes

Building and maintaining a show vehicle is a very large project and can take many hundreds if not thousands of hours to complete (are they ever complete?). When working so closely on such large projects, one may be too close or too familiar with the vehicle that some details may be overlooked. Getting others to look at your vehicle with a fresh perspective can reveal items you may never have noticed yourself.

When you have someone else look over your vehicle, have them score it as if they were the judge. You may want to give them a copy of the blank sheet that you already received or one you've made up. If not, you could use the sample sheet included in this book. While they're judging, give them space and don't comment on any specific area of what they're scrutinizing. Better yet, go get a cup of coffee and let them do what you've asked without hanging over their shoulder. They should act as if they were the real judge. Give them instructions to be objective and accurate in their critique and not to pull any punches. This isn't a personal attack, it is meant to be constructive.

Another way to get some more input is to use your club or join a club if you're not already a member. These folks are a great resource and usually love to talk about their hobby. They also may have an enormous amount experience that you can leverage. You could get together with a number of other members and have each one rate the others. This way you get more than one score sheet for your vehicle. Have a discussion after the judging to hear the the comments of the others. See what they think beyond the score sheet. This can be a good reason to simply get together and have some good old fashioned bench racing. Try to stay away from personal preferences and stick to discussion around quality. Issues of style should probably be avoided as those may get too personal for some folks.

Location Location Location

Many events have no specified location for where you will place your vehicle. If you have a choice, get a location where you're at the center of the action as well as where the audience will be looking. This is very important when in people's choice events. You can be too close to the center of the action and you may be ignored because you're in the way of the band or some other attraction. I recommend staying away from the restrooms. Even though they will get a lot of foot traffic, the goal of that traffic isn't necessarily to view your vehicle.

Learn More

One thing that I keep running into is that there is always more to learn. There is always someone else who either knows more or knows different things than you do. An excellent question to ask is how is 'it' done by others. It doesn't matter what 'it' is, just that you're seeking out the wisdom and experience of others who have gone before you. It seems that everyone I've talked to have their own specific tips and techniques for getting ready for a show. I've had to do this type of information gathering for this book. I've talked with folks who have decades of judging experience in various capacities.

Research information on your specific car. This could be related to details that will help in a stock class and you want to make sure every nut, bolt, and manufacturing mark is exactly as it was when originally leaving the factory. Your information may be specific to modified classes as in finding more current and innovative techniques for implementing various vehicle systems.

Whatever the case may be, continually gather all the knowledge you can and use it to your advantage. Research is a term that implies work. Fortunately this is a fun hobby and the 'work' you'll be performing is simply more fun.

Gather information by looking at other cars. Look at how they are presented, how they have refinished or restored or modified their vehicles to get ideas. Copy with pride and add your own style. This hobby is an ever changing one and there will always be something new and cool. Take your camera along when looking at details because there will be a lot. Don't take pictures of only the cool cars, take pictures for a purpose. I've used my camera many times to take pictures of wheels, factory labels, show registration cards, part identifications and other things to reference later. The goal of these pictures is for data gathering. This is a simple way of remembering a technique or idea without the need for writing it down or worse yet, trying to remember.

One last item here is to learn more about detailing. There are a number of excellent resources on this topics such as books and web sites. Talk with other enthusiasts and find out their special tricks for cleaning. I can't stress enough that the detail job performed on a vehicle goes a long way with the judges. This is also an area where you can easily pick up or lose points. A missed spot of dirt or wax residue will likely be spotted and will be deducted.

Top Down Approach

Finally, when approaching the items that you need to remedy for the next event, be organized and plan ahead. Make a list of all the items you need to address and put them in order. You may want to order by cost or amount of time and labor that is involved. You may want to order it by the items that are the most obvious detractors and remedying them will give the biggest bang for the buck.

Once you have the list, start from the top, and work your way down. Checking items off a list as well as knowing that your

How to Improve

vehicle is attaining higher quality with each item is a satisfying feeling. Focus on the easiest and cheapest first while working toward the difficult and expensive. Some items may never be addressed because of the difficulty or cost or just that your goals include driving your vehicle more than showing and a perfectly painted chassis is not worth the effort.

Each item in this list of ways to improve your vehicle is a step in a process that should be repeated for each event and hopefully the list of addressable items will continually get smaller. The idea is much like a sculpture, keep shaving away the items that detract and work toward revealing quality and perfection.

Prepare To Be Judged

Hosting a Clinic

I've talked with lots of folks about the various topics covered in this book and even the most seasoned car show participant is surprised at the range of detail that show judges will inspect. There are also many car owners out there that believe their vehicle isn't good enough for a judged show and may be rejected or possibly worse, laughed out of the show. They may also be intimidated by the perceived level of cars that they see at shows and don't think they're up to the task of competing. Another possibility is that they simply don't know how the shows work and are unfamiliar with the standard practices and don't know where to get the information to alleviate their fears and anxieties.

Participating in these events primarily should be fun with the competition friendly. We're all out here to promote and enjoy our past time as well as push the standard of creativity and execution to new levels. We want as many people as possible to become a participant and enjoy all that the hobby has to offer without reservation.

One way to remove much of that hesitancy is to host a clinic and break down those barriers. I believe that a great way to reduce or even remove fear is by greater understanding and knowledge. The more I know about a topic, the more confidence I have in being involved with that topic. Hosting a show clinic is an excellent way to bring folks up to speed.

You might think that to host a clinic would imply that you're either involved in hosting a show or a show promoter but that isn't required. There are a number of groups that might want to host a get-together like this. A clinic could be arranged as a club event simply for a time to get together. You might be so inspired by this book that you'll want to get a group of friends together so you can pass along all your newly found knowledge.

What are the Benefits

There are a number of benefits to hosting a clinic aside from the obvious, especially if you are a promoter. The first is that the spectators will be given a better show and have more enjoyment while they attend. Shows are hosted for a number of reasons from simply having some fun to fund-raising and all the way to a for-profit venture. In all of these cases, the spectators, whether they're also participants or not, are a major component of increasing the popularity of the show. Why will they attend if not for the high quality of vehicles that they come to see?

The second benefit is for the participants themselves. Not only will you, as the promoter, come across as more welcoming, but you will also lower some of the barriers for being a participant in the first place. Both new participants and old veterans who think they've seen it all will benefit and hopefully learn something new. Even a poorly hosted clinic is beneficial because it will convey the main idea of focusing on the details and may spark new ideas by what you've said for things you didn't even cover. They'll then be able to maximize their vehicle, compete better, and gain more confidence in their ability to show.

The final benefit is for the promoters themselves. This is a venue

Hosting a Clinic

where you can bring new participants in and show them the ins and outs of your show as well as how they can improve. The main benefit is that by increasing the quality of the vehicles and helping the participants, you will draw a bigger crowd that will enjoy the show more, which will in turn draw more and better participants, and so on. All of these benefits will help you attain and push further the goals you have for your show. Of course this isn't the only element of a good show, but like I've said many times already, focus on all the details and everything will benefit.

What to Include

The contents of your clinic should be tailored to the show you're hosting. There are many types of shows, rules to abide by, safety standards to be followed and methods of judging, all of which you'll want to cover at some level. The goal is not to cover how to prepare for a show but how to prepare for your show at a level that is appropriate. You want to cover the topics but don't get bogged down in those details while not leaving enough time to cover the meat of the clinic.

After discussing the specifics of your show, you'll want to present an overview of how to prepare at a high level and then dive deeper into each of the specific topics to give adequate time for each. An easy way to be sure to cover all the pertinent topics is to start with an outline. A good one to follow can be found in the table of contents of this book. You don't need to present a book report, but it's likely that you already have some show experience as well as having read this book and will understand the topics I've covered.

Depending on the way your show is run, you'll want to discuss the issues you've seen most often by previous participants that could easily be remedied. Include the criteria used by your judges (if you have them) and how they perform their task. There may be some specifics to your show that would help participants be better prepared.

Keep the clinic specific and relevant to your show. Talk about what you've seen before both good and bad and give plenty of examples. Try to do this for all the categories you cover if possible. If you have pictures that you can show to help drive home your points, present those as well. As they say, a picture is worth a thousand words. Try to keep the images high quality so they will actually help the participants and not confuse them. Be specific with the images presented and don't include any simply because you had pictures to show. You want to convey a clear message in a limited amount of time, use that time wisely.

A word of caution with the pictures that you may include in your presentation. Take care to be sensitive to the vehicle owner of the photos and don't embarrass them. Be careful with what you say and stay relevant to the topic and refrain from any personal comments. The car hobby community is fairly well connected and you never know who might be listening.

One last item to include that may or may not be obvious is to allow time for questions and answers. No matter how prepared you are or how well you've covered the material, you are looking at the clinic from your perspective and others will have their own. There will almost always be some topic that hasn't been covered well enough, or at all, and this is the time to clarify or supplement. It is also a good time to have a pen and paper handy to take your own notes for any future clinics you may hold.

Since you've gained so much wisdom in creating your material and helping all those current and future show participants, be sure to recommend that they get their own copy of this book so they can get greater knowledge and insight for preparing for the next show.

When to have the Clinic

When a clinic is to be presented while it is associated with a specific show, there are a couple of times when you might want to have it scheduled. You could have it before or during the show itself. This probably is a bit obvious but you'll want to consider your show and its intended participants when scheduling the

Hosting a Clinic

event.

Is the show professionally judged or less competitive in nature? Are the spectators a paying audience or simply an ad-hoc crowd of folks who show up? Are the participants pre-registered or can they show up any time during the day of the show? Do the participants have to pay to enter or do they simply show up and park? Is the show affiliated with a specific club or other type of organization which implies its own rules or is this just a casual get-together for those who like cars? All of these questions and probably many others will help to determine whether to have the clinic before or during the event.

If you schedule your clinic before the show, make sure there is enough time prior to the show where participants can implement what they've learned but not too much time so that they forget. If the clinic is during the show, make it a highlight of the show and promote it like you would if you were having a special guest attend like Chip Foose.

Whenever you decide to schedule the clinic, make it a valuable part of the show since we've already discussed that there are benefits to everyone involved.

Organization

A clinic is like any other presentation whether that be a simple budget report from a local club to a motivational speech, to a sermon, to a state of the union address by high ranking officials. All of them are attempting to present a clear and meaningful message for their audience and some do this much better than others.

The key to getting your message across is being organized. Have a plan or outline of what you want to cover, stick to and execute the plan and don't include unnecessary or confusing messages. This of course doesn't mean that you shouldn't be funny or have amusing stories, those things are the grease that makes the clinic flow and be more meaningful.

Prepare To Be Judged

Along with what you present and how it is presented, the presenter should also be chosen appropriately when possible. Find someone who has a passion for shows and the cars that are part of them; someone who likes to talk with show participants and has some experience. This will give more credibility to their message even if they didn't create it themselves. Present the material in a fun and friendly manner to help the participants increase their confidence in showing their vehicle. A list of strict rules that are presented by a control freak droning on and on about what not to do won't help anyone.

No matter what you include in your clinic, how you present it, or who presents it, if you're working for the benefit of the participants, spectators, and you the promoter, you'll succeed in your aim. There are a lot of assumptions made when getting ready for a show and giving guidance and detailed information to the car owners will do nothing but benefit the whole hobby.

Sample Score Sheet

Usage

Typically a judged show will have a number of categories that each vehicle is measured against. These can include body, paint, engine, chassis, interior and safety among a number of others. Some shows start with a maximum possible score and deduct points as imperfections are found. Others start with zero points and increase when scores are given. This sample sheet will give you a good starting point for evaluating your own vehicle. Assume each item is worth a maximum of 5 points.

Body

_____ Body Condition and Detail

_____ Panel Fit

_____ Accessories

Prepare To Be Judged

____ Grille

____ Trim

____ Hood (bonnet)

____ Fenders

____ Trunk (boot)

____ Headlights

____ Taillights

____ Brightwork

Paint

____ Factory/Custom Graphics

____ Authenticity/Originality/Creativity

____ Condition and Detail

____ Hidden Areas

____ Paint Sub-Total

Engine

____ Authenticity/Originality/Creativity

____ Engineering

____ Factory Equipment

____ Wiring

____ Plumbing (brake, fuel, heating/cooling)

____ Plating, Finishes, and Brightwork

____ Detail

____ Engine Sub-Total

Chassis

____ Frame / Underside

Sample Score Sheet

____ Engineering

____ Front Suspension/Steering, Brakes, etc.

____ Rear Suspension/Rear End, Brakes, etc.

____ Driveline

____ Brightwork

____ Exhaust System

____ Factory/Custom Finish and Detail including Hidden Areas

____ Wheels and Tires – Indexed and Detailed

____ Chassis Sub-Total

Interior

____ Seating, Panels, and Headliner

____ Dash and Console

____ Floor Coverings

____ Brightwork

____ Convertible Top

____ Windows, Trim, and Weatherstripping

____ Trunk (boot) or Bed

____ Condition and Detail

____ Interior Sub-Total

Safety

____ Factory or Custom Equipment

____ Condition and Detail

____ Safety Sub-Total

Display

____ Judge's Book

Prepare To Be Judged

____ Story Board

____ Is there a Display?

____ Display Sub-Total

____ Total Points

Pointers

Clean, polish, dust, remove bugs, clean windows, clean weatherstripping, clean cat's whiskers, and detail all nooks and crannies. Open the hood, open a door, open the trunk, put the top up if convertible, detail the whole body, detail emblems, search for missed dirt, and clean all polishing residue. Engine should be dirt and grease free, all finishes cleaned and polished, wiring and plumbing should be clean and routed appropriately. Chassis should have no leaks, oil, or dirt. The tires should be fully cleaned including tread and the wheels cleaned even on the back side and don't forget to index. Detail the trunk and remove everything from the vehicle that didn't come with it such as folding chairs or cleaning supplies. Have a judge's book that highlights the details of your vehicle or history. A simple display sends the message that completes the package.

If you attend to all the details, you'll position yourself ahead of most everyone else. Very few go this far.

Afterword

Like most of you, I love cars. Cars of all types and styles. I'm an equal opportunity enthusiast. I do gravitate toward a few particular manufacturers, but truly, I have a great appreciation for many vehicles, especially old ones. Whenever I'm traveling the countryside, I constantly have an eye watching out for the derelict under the tree or the old hulk sitting in a field or a tantalizing shape under a tarp in a garage being used as a storage shelf.

When I see an old car or truck sitting neglected in some out of the way place, where most folks might just see some old rusty hunk of steel, I start thinking about the history of the vehicle including how it ended up where it is, what caused it to stop being a useful form of transport, and what it was like when it new. My mind then starts picturing what that vehicle could and I start evaluating how far gone it truly is and what take to resurrect it to either its former glory or to so totally new and wonderful.

Prepare To Be Judged

I've been looking at cars in this fashion for as long as I can remember and something occurred to me not too long ago relating to this concept. I realized that the way I view old junker vehicles is the same way that God views all of us. God isn't a contemptuous God who wants to punish us. He is a loving and gracious God and wants to restore and renew our lives and have a personal relationship with us. I also realized that this is the way He wants me to view and treat other people. I pray that God will help me with this ability, since it doesn't come naturally. It will be a lifetime journey of growth.

Like with an old car or truck, I don't have any personal hatred toward the vehicle because of the rust, stains, or damage. They are simply defects that need to be dealt with so the beauty of the vehicle is allowed to shine. God holds the same view of us, no malice, just loving kindness and a willingness to care for us in spite of our faults. He has the ability to renew and restore us. Fortunately, God doesn't entertain the idea of 'too far gone' relating to people the way I might when looking at an old car or truck.

In a judged car show, your vehicle doesn't necessarily have to be perfect to win first place, you only have to be better than those around you. This is sort of like being graded on a curve. From God's perspective, life isn't graded on a curve, though many people look at it that way. They may feel "I'm a good person, I haven't gone to jail, I haven't committed any major crimes, I should be accepted". The fallacy of this logic is that they're comparing themselves with themselves and others they know or see around them. They, along with everyone else with this view, have their own differing opinions of 'good enough'. Their view of 'good enough' is based on how they feel or what they think ˜d not on a standardized scale.

Uı˛

vehicthe premise of this book where you have to prepare your of the priḥ excruciating detail prior to being judged worthy to get your ĩnd wants you to come to Him *before* you attempt your own (just ınrder because there is nothing you can do on ˜ur car can't on its own) to be worthy of

Afterword

the prize. You'll never measure up to His standard (perfection), none of us will. The good news is that God provided a way to be judged worthy and to be extended grace. That is to recognize that you, like me and everyone else, aren't perfect and don't measure up to the standard. You then simply accept that His son Jesus died as a sacrifice to pay for our faults and rose to live again because death held no lasting power over him. This is a free gift.

Life is really graded as pass/fail and the creator of the universe holds the standard to which everyone is measured. As with car shows, the only opinion that counts is from the one that is doing the judging. In life, there is only one way to pass and that is to accept the gift that God has given.

If you have any questions on this or any other part of the book, please contact me, I'd love to hear from you.

http://thepistonhead.com

Prepare To Be Judged